India

MANAGING EDITORS
Amy Bauman
Barbara J. Behm

CONTENT EDITORS
Amanda Barrickman
James I. Clark
Patricia Lantier
Charles P. Milne, Jr.
Katherine C. Noonan
Christine Snyder
Gary Turbak
William M. Vogt
Denise A. Wenger
Harold L. Willis
John Wolf

ASSISTANT EDITORS
Ann Angel
Michelle Dambeck
Barbara Murray
Renee Prink
Andrea J. Schneider

INDEXER
James I. Clark

ART/PRODUCTION
Suzanne Beck, Art Director
Andrew Rupniewski, Production Manager
Eileen Rickey, Typesetter

Library of Congress Number: 88-18337

2 3 4 5 6 7 8 9 0   97 96 95 94 93 92

Library of Congress Cataloging-in-Publication Data

Massa, Renato
  [India. English]
  India / Renato Massa.

  — (World nature encyclopedia)
  Translation of: India.
  Includes index.
  Summary: Describes the plant and animal life of India and
its interaction with the environment.
  1. Ecology—India—Juvenile literature. 2. Biotic
communities—India—Juvenile literature. [1. Ecology—
India. 2. India.] I. Title. II. Series: Natura nel mondo.
English.
QH183.M27 1988 574.5′264′0954—dc19   88-18384
ISBN 0-8172-3325-3

WORLD NATURE ENCYCLOPEDIA

India

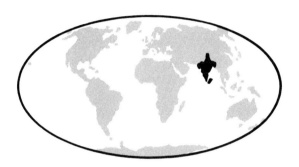

Renato Massa

RAINTREE
STECK-VAUGHN
L I B R A R Y

Austin, Texas

CONTENTS

INTRODUCTION

The Indian subcontinent is an immense triangle of land with an area of 1.5 million square miles (3.9 million square kilometers), equal to 40 percent of all of Europe. It lies between the largest mountain chain in the world, the Himalayas, and one of the largest tropical bodies of water, the Indian Ocean. The Indian subcontinent includes India, the southern part of Nepal, Bangladesh, Pakistan, and the island-nation of Sri Lanka. It makes up nearly half the western part of the vast Indo-Malaysian region. This region is one of the major biogeographical (referring to the geographic distribution of plants and animals) groupings of the earth.

The northern limits of the subcontinent largely coincide with the borders of India. The western limit is the Indus River in the territory of Pakistan, and the eastern limit is the delta of the Ganges River. This book, however, for reasons of biogeographical uniformity, deals with a smaller area. It excludes the highest part of

the Himalayas as well as the deserts of northwestern India and Pakistan. The area included is considered one of the most fascinating regions of the world.

Certain features described in the writings of the Greek historian Herodotus (fifth century B.C.) can still be observed in the Indian social system and its traditions. Originally, the Indian languages and religions had a strong influence on the different languages and religions of the people who inhabited the areas around the Mediterranean Sea. India is more than a refuge of the last yogis (people who practice yoga), fakirs (people who perform feats of magic or endurance), hermits, and enthusiasts of the Hindu religion that survive on the planet. It is also an extraordinary natural universe of wildlife. Thanks to the efforts of many writers and explorers, it has become well known throughout the world.

THE INDIAN SUBCONTINENT

Geography and Geology

The Indo-Malaysian region began to take its present physical shape about 63 million years ago. The first raising of land, which formed the Himalayas, occurred approximately 25 million years ago. Before that period, which is called the Miocene epoch, India was a large island moving toward the north. As it reached and linked up with the rest of Asia, the spectacular Himalayan chain was formed.

There mountains, the most majestic in the world, separate India from central Asia. There is no barrier to the west where arid Pakistani territory begins. Nor is there to the east, where evergreen forests and mangrove swamps are mixed with the vegetation characteristic of the Indo-Chinese peninsula.

Within the vast triangle of the Indian peninsula lies another triangular area, the Deccan plateau. This is separated from the Himalayas by the vast plains of the Indus and Ganges rivers. Generally, the Deccan plateau does not exceed 3,280 feet (1,000 meters) in elevation. It borders the following mountain chains: the Western Ghats, which reach 8,698 feet (2,652 m); the Eastern Ghats, which are a little higher than 3,280 feet (1,000 m); and the Satpura, Vindhya, and Maikala mountain chains, which reach 10,496 feet (3,200 m) in elevation. Beyond the Western and Eastern Ghats, there are two narrow coastal strips that originally were flood plains. The western coast is called Malabar, and the eastern one is Coromandel.

From a geological point of view, the island of Sri Lanka is part of the Indian subcontinent, although it is separated from India by the Palk Strait. The island has a low plain to the north and a mountain chain, dominated by Adam's Peak and the Pidurutalaga mountain, to the south.

Climate

The climate of the vast Indian subregion is dominated by monsoons, which are winds that blow regularly from south to north, then vice versa. Just before the beginning of summer, when the sun is over the Tropic of Cancer, a large low-pressure area forms in northern India. The humid ocean air then moves toward the north, sweeping over the dry earth and dropping torrential rain. This is fortunate because, just prior to

Opposite page: The snowy peak of Annapurna is one of the highest in the Himalayas at 26,500 feet (8,078 m). It is also one of the better-known mountains among mountain climbers who use Kathmandu as a base. The large chain of the Himalayas separates the northern part of the Indian region from the rest of the Asian subcontinent.

Diagram of the formation of the summer monsoon (*left*) and the winter monsoon (*right*). At the beginning of the summer, when the rays of the sun are vertical over the tropic of Cancer, a low-pressure area is created in the northern areas of India that attracts humid air from the ocean. A mass of humid air crosses India from south to north, resulting in heavy rainfall on all the Indian subcontinent. In winter, the rays of the sun are vertical over another area, the tropic of Capricorn. The humid air is then attracted to the south (Malaysia and Indonesia), leaving the Indian subcontinent very dry for several months.

this time, India becomes one of the hottest and driest areas in the world.

The naturalist Pierre Pfeffer writes: "During the month of May, in Calcutta, the thermometer reaches 113° Fahrenheit (45° Celsius). People collapse in the street from sunstroke, and under the trees along the avenues one finds crows, parakeets, and giant fruit bats that have been killed by the heat. When the rains arrive, they are usually so violent that the Indians speak of them as 'explosions of the monsoon,' and the people become delirious with joy. The air is purified, and people and animals once more breathe freely, even though the temperature in Calcutta is still higher than the temperature of most European and North American climates during the hottest parts of the summer. Naked children play in the rain, animals roll happily in the puddles, and the parched earth absorbs the water."

In the winter, the sun is over the Tropic of Capricorn, thousands of miles south of the Indo-Malaysian region. A new low-pressure area forms. As a

sun rays

sun rays

result, besides the summer monsoon (which actually arrives in late spring), India also experiences a winter monsoon. Unlike the summer monsoon, the winter one blows from north to south.

Moving from north to south, the fresh air of central Asia initially brings a dry and pleasant autumn. It eventually carries away all the humidity, releasing it over Malaysia and Indonesia for many months. The rains are unequally distributed. As much as 79 to 118 inches (2,000 to 3,000 millimeters) of rain may fall annually on the Malabar coast. Sometimes as much as 236 inches (6,000 mm) of rain fall in the northeast area in the Assam region. To the northwest, along the Indus valley, there is a lower annual rainfall. In several localities in this area, the annual rainfall is only 3.9 inches (100 mm). This is typical of the most arid zones of the world.

The Himalayan Zone

Elevation, rainfall, and other local factors result in a series of climate and vegetation zones that often overlap to form an intricate mosaic. There is a great difference between the Himalayan zone and the peninsular zone. The Himalayan zone includes the northern-

The arrival of the monsoon on the beach of Sri Lanka is greeted with joy. The rains it brings are important to farm crops. However, the monsoon rains do not fall equally throughout the region. The first obstacles rain clouds from the ocean encounter are the coastal mountains, where the largest amount of rainfall is dropped in downpours. As the monsoon proceeds farther into India, the rainfall is lessened and its intensity is decreased. The monsoons are also subject to variations in intensity in different years. The amount of rainfall dropped is not always enough to guarantee an adequate harvest.

11

mango

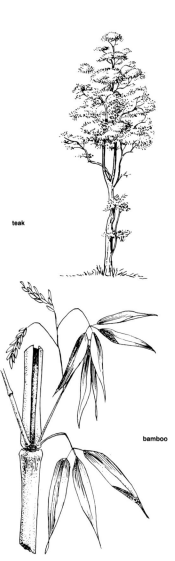
teak

bamboo

most part of the Indian subcontinent up to the Indus and the Brahmaputra rivers. The second zone covers the entire peninsula.

The Himalayan zone can, in turn, be divided into a subzone of forests and a Tibetan subzone. Up to an elevation of 4,920 feet (1,500 m), the forests are mostly made up of tropical species of trees and plants. These include sal and silk-cotton trees, as well as giant bamboos. In elevations from 4,920 to 9,840 feet (1,500 to 3,000 m), the forests have a more "temperate" character. They are made up of oak, magnolia, laurel, and birch trees, covered with mosses and ferns. Beyond 9,840 to 11,480 feet (3,000 to 3,500 m), the forests are those of typical mountainous regions. There are many pine and larch trees with an undergrowth of rhododendrons and dwarf bamboo.

The animal life of this temperate, or colder, zone is quite different from that of the rest of India. Although there is a scarcity of many tropical species, Chinese and Indo-Chinese species are found here that do not exist in the rest of India.

The plateau of Tibet is very different from the subzone of the forests. This area, along with eastern Ladakh, can be described as one of the few regions of the world where arctic and desert conditions exist at the same time. This region has extraordinary variety from a biological point of view and deserves special attention.

In the Kashmir and the Western Ladakh regions, the conditions of the Himalayan forests gradually become more "peninsular." In the eastern Himalayan area, one finds a clear transition toward European conditions. Above 28° north latitude, one finds such "Nordic" animals as moles, shrew mice, magpies, marmots, and musk deer. South of this line, the forests are populated by giant fruit bats, large squirrels, mongooses, tree shrews, and civet cats.

The Peninsular Zone

The peninsular zone of India can be divided into a desert subzone in the northwest, a subzone of the Ganges River plain, a subzone corresponding to the triangle of the Deccan plateau, and a subzone corresponding to the Malabar coast.

The first of these four subzones is located in the Rajasthan region. This area is the eastern limit of the

This map shows the vegetation in India. The true evergreen rain forests are limited to several coastal strips. Then one finds various types of dry deciduous forests. Proceeding toward the Himalayas, one finds conifer (evergreen) forests similar to those in Europe. This map does not take into account the changes in the vegetation due to deforestation.

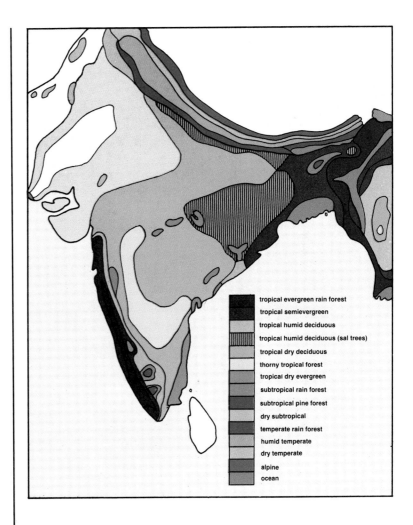

tropical evergreen rain forest
tropical semievergreen
tropical humid deciduous
tropical humid deciduous (sal trees)
tropical dry deciduous
thorny tropical forest
tropical dry evergreen
subtropical rain forest
subtropical pine forest
dry subtropical
temperate rain forest
humid temperate
dry temperate
alpine
ocean

vast desert region that extends across western Asia. It begins in the Mediterranean area of Saudi Arabia and extends across Iran, Iraq, Afghanistan, and Pakistan.

The Ganges River plain becomes more humid in the eastern part. In the Bengal region, it becomes a wide, green strip of mango, palm, and fig trees. In the area of the Ganges delta, there is a humid tangle of forests, grasses, and mangrove swamps.

The vast Deccan triangle, which covers a large part of the peninsula, is a region of moderate rainfall. The vegetation is not lush. It includes thorny acacia trees and small trees and bushes that lose all their leaves in the dry season. Here and there one finds a forest of hardwoods dominated by teak trees. These forests have an appearance that is strangely similar to the broad-leaved forests of the temperate zones of the earth.

A field of rice is tended in Sri Lanka. On the Indian subcontinent, the energy necessary for farm work is largely provided by oxen and buffalo. The buffalo have been domesticated for thousands of years. They are particularly useful in the marshy areas, where they can easily move around. They are also resistant to parasites and disease. In the photo, one can see several white herons, two crows, and a gray heron. They are interested spectators who patiently wait for the plow to uncover worms and other invertebrates.

Black soil is found in the area between the cities of Goa, Bombay, Indore, and Nagpur. This soil comes from basaltic lavas, and it helps make the area suitable for growing cotton. West of the city of Nagpur, the volcanic rock formations are covered by crystalline rocks and blocks of sandstone. The soils that developed from these rocks result in a more humid forest dominated by bamboo and sal trees.

The area south of the Deccan plateau suddenly rises up in the location of the Nilgiri, Anaimalai, and Pulni mountains. These form a series of terraces and grassy hills separated by valleys covered with evergreen forests. The Indian people call these forested valleys "sholas." The sholas have many features in common with the animals and vegetation of the Malabar coastal zone and the Western Ghats, which separate the Malabar area from the Deccan area. It is very humid, and abundant rain falls throughout the year.

Pictured is a suburban zone in southern India. To meet the needs of a growing population, a large part of the Indian territory has been deforested and used for farming. India is now experiencing more poverty in the suburban areas, which lack all services and utilities. Well-known Indian wildlife is disappearing from these areas, leaving only domestic animals and several wild animals that are adapted to living off the refuse of humans.

Dense and beautiful evergreen forests that resemble those of Indochina abound in this region. As a result, in these zones one finds animals that are basically of a "tropical" type. Some of them are found only in limited geographic areas. For example, a certain type of monkey is found only in the Nilgiri area, and a certain type of civet cat is found only in the Malabar area. Other animals that live in restricted areas are the brown mongoose with a striped neck, the spiny mouse, and the macaco monkey. Many of the same animals that populate the monsoon forest and the bushy savannas also live in these areas.

The Effects of Humans

Today, the Indian subcontinent is one of the most populated areas of the earth. Counting all the inhabitants of the various countries that compose the subcontinent, the population exceeds 800 million people. In India alone, in 1988, the population was estimated at 816 million. Because of the large population, one would not expect to find the savannas, rain forests, coasts with mangrove trees, or any other natural environments that are a part of this subcontinent.

THE ANIMALS OF DELHI

Waking up in the city of Delhi for the first time is an unforgettable experience. The sky, the buildings, the streets, the gardens, and the trees all present a tropical atmosphere. If you arrive in autumn or winter, you will find morning air that is fresh but not biting. At the first light of dawn, the most insistent sounds will be those of people singing in the temples, a sound amplified by loudspeakers. You will also hear the harsh sounds of crows that are everywhere, moving from branch to branch and coming down to the streets in search of food.

Crows and Starlings

The crows are gray and black in color. They are a bit smaller, but much more bothersome, than the gray crow commonly found in Europe. The zoologist that first described these crows called them "splendent," probably as a joke. The Indians call them "house crows," to distinguish them from the large, black "jungle crows," which are not as closely associated with the activities of humans.

The crows are everywhere in the city of Delhi, as they are in every city of India and Sri Lanka. They feed on all kinds of garbage. They let people get very close to them, and, in the public gardens, they will even rush up and take food from the hands of people. They are always found in large numbers on the busiest streets of the city, together with sparrows, mynas, and squirrels, trying to make off with some peanuts, pumpkin seeds, or cereal grains of street vendors.

The only birds that are more bothersome than crows, and which interact more with humans, are the common mynas. They belong to the same family as the European starlings, which they resemble in size and shape. They are gray and black in color and are smaller than crows in size. These birds are characterized by two fleshy, yellow folds of skin behind the eyes. The mynas waddle everywhere in search of garbage. They even go so far as to land on bar tables or inside stopped buses to gather the remains of scanty meals left there.

Mynas are always found in groups of at least two, and often they gather in huge flocks. They are easy to spot in flight because they have many white spots on their wings, and the edge of their tail is pure white.

Like the starlings of the temperate regions, the common Indian mynas quickly adapted to their environ-

Opposite page: A Bengala vulture roosts on a dead branch. These spectacular and majestic animals are scavengers. They gather in large numbers not only where there are carcasses but also near garbage dumps and food markets. Their high population density in several Indian cities is due to the proximity of humans. They would never be as numerous under natural conditions.

17

In India, the common myna is the most widespread representative of the starling family. Both male and female mynas have a varied call, much like the starlings of the temperate regions of Eurasia. The call is a combination of harsh sounds, whistles, and imitations. The imitating abilities of the myna are not as great as those of the religious grackle. This similar but larger bird of the starling family is found only in forests. The grackle can whistle entire melodies and repeat words. Because of this ability, the religious grackle has been widely sold commercially.

ment. They have also been introduced by humans even in areas far away from their native India and have spread over great distances. These areas include the entire Indochina territory, South Africa, Madagascar, Australia, New Zealand, and various islands in the Pacific Ocean.

Besides the common mynas, one finds two other kinds of starlings in Delhi. One is the variegated myna, which is white and black with a patch of reddish orange skin around the eyes. The second type is the pagoda myna. It is smaller, with a gray-colored backside, chestnut-colored cheeks and breast, and a black head topped by a long, erect crest. Both of these kinds of

mynas are usually seen, in pairs or in small groups, in the gardens and lawns of the city. Although they are almost as trusting of humans as the common starlings, they do not often venture forth into the streets.

Vultures and Kites

The enormous amount of refuse left in the streets provides food for other birds that are much more spectacular and unusual than starlings and crows. These are the brown kites and various kinds of vultures. In the city of Delhi alone, there are at least two thousand nesting pairs of kites.

All these birds of prey have developed local habits Western people consider unusual. A Westerner would think that these birds of prey would be unapproachable and wild and that they would keep more space between themselves and other birds. However, in Delhi, the brown kites roost on the roofs of houses and on tree branches and come down to the streets without fear to feed on all kinds of refuse.

The vultures can be seen by the tens and hundreds on the branches of certain trees and on old buildings. They can also be seen flying slowly above the markets and open areas in their search for food scraps. They may happen upon scraps from a butcher, the carcass of a dog that has been hit by a car, or a cow that has just died.

Small Mammals

Alongside these winged refuse eaters, one finds small mammals, such as rats, mice, and squirrels. The squirrels are either three-striped or five-striped and are widespread throughout all of India. The five-striped squirrel is more common in the northern part of the country, while the three-striped squirrel is more common in the south.

At this time, the five-striped squirrels have become as dependent on humans as the mice and rats. In the cities one can see them on trees and in gardens, as well as on the eaves of houses and on low walls. They are found wherever there is a possibility of finding something to eat. Although the three-striped squirrels are a little more wary of humans, in some areas they are found in the same environments as the five-striped animals.

Among the other small mammals that inhabit the city, one finds the musk shrew, which is a type of mouse.

The musk shrew is about 4 to 6 inches (10 to 15 centimeters) long and is insectivorous, which means it feeds on insects.

The Indian musk shrew often gets inside houses, where it can be easily mistaken for a mouse. It is not hard to recognize, however, because its body is long and thin and resembles that of a tiny weasel. The musk shrew has a pointed snout which is very important during the search for food. The shrew pokes the point of its snout into every corner of the house, as if it were sniffing out the trail of some insect.

Parrots in the City

Many other animals live in close association with humans in Delhi. The city has a large population of animals that is not always as visible or as trusting of humans as the refuse eaters already discussed.

One of the most visible animals in the sky of the Indian capital is the collared parakeet. This is a bright

The five-striped squirrel and the pagoda starling are among the most typical animals found in Indian gardens and parks. As with the people in central and northern Europe, the people of India are protective of this squirrel as well as other little animals. They feed them in the city parks and streets. For this reason, many species are not afraid of humans, and they can be easily observed almost everywhere.

green parrot, the size of a dove but with a longer tail. The collared parakeets are found in noisy groups all over the city and are easily recognized by their loud sounds and long tails. They roost on buildings and nest in the holes of old walls and in trees but, unlike the other birds, they do not get too close to people.

These exotic birds are captured in large numbers and sold as pets. It would seem that the noisy groups of parrots in Delhi are aware of this practice. In fact, one can observe a large flock of them noisily entering the foliage of a tree and immediately vanishing behind the leaves. As soon as they roost, the parakeets become silent and move slowly from branch to branch, swaying like large leaves in the wind. Finding them under these conditions is not easy, even if one sees them arrive and knows that among the leaves of a certain tree there may be ten or twenty of these birds.

The Alexandrian parakeet is also found in city parks. It can be recognized by its larger size, a

The collared parakeet is the most common species of parrot in the Indian subcontinent. It is also the easiest to observe in urban environments. Despite its familiarity with humans, the collared parakeet is considerably more cautious than other birds of the city. This is due to the fact that for centuries these birds have been captured, exported, and sold as caged pets. Recently, some of these pets that have escaped in Europe have started to reproduce in the wild. This has occurred in England and Italy, where they seem to have adjusted well.

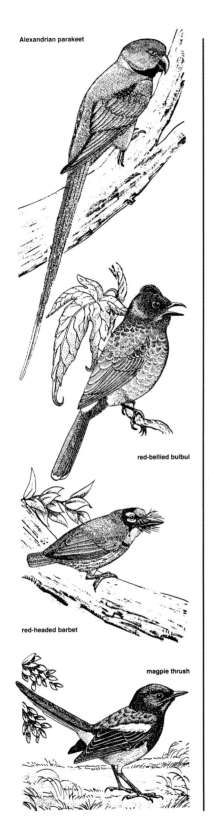

Alexandrian parakeet

red-bellied bulbul

red-headed barbet

magpie thrush

chestnut-colored spot on the wings, and by its purple head. The male of the species has a head that is a beautiful lilac color, and its tail is even longer than the tail of the collared parakeet. Its call is more musical, which makes it easily recognizable even in flight and from long distances.

Songbirds

The city of Delhi offers other exotic parakeets to the visitor who is interested in ornithology (the study of birds). A bird-watcher can find many types of small songbirds here that have never been seen in the gardens of Europe. For example, there is the bulbul, which is about the size of a large bunting. This bird has a crest of feathers and a unique, musical call. There are many species of this bird, but the most common types are the bulbuls with red bellies, the bulbuls with red cheeks, and the bulbuls with white cheeks.

Similar to the blackbird in size and shape, these birds are primarily gray, with attractive, bright yellow eyes. They move about in groups of three to seven, following each other with movements that are unlike those of blackbirds. The chirping sound of the bulbuls is very loud.

These birds belong to the family Timaliids, which has an unusual type of social system that is well known to ethologists (people who study animal behavior). The social ties between the group are so strong that they are still maintained even when two birds of the group pair off and nest. In this situation, the other birds of the group act as helpers in gathering food for the newly hatched offspring.

Numerous species of thrushes are also found throughout India, and, in Delhi, there are several representatives of the thrush family. For example, there is the magpie thrush, with a beautiful black-and-white coloring and a soft, musical song. This bird is commonly seen in many gardens.

Another is the Indian robin, the male of which is almost completely black, except for bright chestnut-colored feathers behind the abdomen, or belly. This patch of color is plainly visible because of this bird's frequent habit of raising its tail feathers, which may represent some sort of territorial signal.

The black sparrow is another common bird in the

A male peafowl takes flight. This splendid bird originally inhabited only the forests. Today, it has adapted to living also in large suburban parks and farming zones that have a minimum amount of cover vegetation. For this reason, it is still common and widespread. Peafowl often can be observed from the windows of a train or bus. One can easily tell if they are near because the male has a loud, mewing call.

city of Delhi and the surrounding area. The sparrow is coal colored and has a long, forked tail. It often roosts on utility and telephone wires, like the swallows, and feeds on large insects that it captures with acrobatic dives. Its long tail helps in these maneuvers by providing balance.

Another type of bird commonly found in the capital is the barbet. Barbets are similar to woodpeckers in the shape of their legs and feet and in their beautiful green-and-red coloring. Just like the woodpecker, the barbet prefers tree habitats, nesting in the cavities of trees. The red-headed barbet is approximately 5.5 inches (14 cm) long, and its sound is similar to that of a hammer rapidly and rhythmically striking a piece of metal. Because of the particular musical quality of this sound, an unknowing visitor could mistake it for the sound of an insect.

BIRD PARADISE

A long, grayish blue waterway winds through a flat and unbounded range of aquatic plants. This is the Bharatpur bird sanctuary, which at the beginning of this century the Indian prince Kishan Singh set aside as a preserve for web-footed birds. Bharatpur is the richest reserve for birds in Asia, perhaps in all the world. It is only 125 miles (201 km) from the city of New Delhi and 30 miles (50 km) from the famous historical city of Agra. It covers an area of about 15 square miles (39 sq. km) in a marshy zone that still has a considerable amount of tree cover. Nile acacia trees and other large tropical trees are commonly found here.

Multicolored wood storks, anastoms, exotic ibises, spoonbills, and intrusive cormorants are found alone, in pairs, or in groups on the trees of the reserve. Lightweight jacanas and sultana birds walk over the marsh vegetation, while small and large flocks of many kinds of ducks and geese rise up in flight from the water.

Water and Land Trails

The paradise of Bharatpur is a tangle of flooded forests, marshes, and small savannas, crossed by convenient trails. These trails are made on embankments that are high enough to keep dry almost all the time. The visitor can enter this area by car, bicycle, or on foot. One can walk along these trails for hours and encounter only an occasional ranger or a shepherd.

The habitats that can be visited show a lot of variety. They support an array of birds, such as herons, storks, geese, ducks, cormorants, cranes, parrots, aquatic jays, cuckoos, fish-eating martins, sparrows, shrikes, vultures, and eagles. During the winter, more than 500,000 birds have been counted in this reserve, belonging to 350 different species. The ducks and geese certainly represent the largest number of these birds.

Besides the land paths, one can take several aquatic trails. Flat-bottomed boats are available to the visitor who desires to observe the nesting of the exotic and long-necked birds from closer range. By boat, one can also see many other things, such as a python slithering into the water, disturbed by the unexpected visitors.

Dryness and Monsoons

The Bharatpur reserve is located at about twenty-seven degrees north latitude. The summers are very hot

Opposite page: Indian anastoms, or open-beaked storks, engage in a mating ritual. Anastoms are little known outside the tropical zones of Asia. The anastom is one of the most common large wading birds of the Indian region. Its unique beak resembles that of a nutcracker. The exact function of this beak is not known. It might have to do with the fact that the anastom regularly feeds on large mollusks (shellfish), and it must use its strange beak to open their shells.

This drawing shows several typical marsh birds of India. *From left to right:* the nitticor, which is more common in Europe; the Indian ibis, very similar to the sacred African ibis; the white-necked stork, similar to the white stork; the bronze-winged jacana, with unusually long toes (its female mates with several males and defends her own territory); a demoiselle crane; an Indian goose. These last two birds do not nest in India. They reproduce in an area north of the Himalayas and migrate south to winter in India.

here and, at first, also quite dry. But when the monsoon winds from the southwest begin to blow from the ocean, it becomes increasingly rainy. The rains start in June and last until October. Rainfall is generally abundant, and, at times, it can be extreme and violent. Entire territories can become impassable for months at a time. Because of the weather conditions, only a few species of birds can nest in northern India during the spring season. Many other species wait until the end of the monsoon rains. They start to reproduce in October when water is abundant (and so are the small animals that live in it), the sky is regularly calm, and the nights cool. This is also the case for the smaller animals, who can take advantage of the longer periods of daylight to search for food for the young while the food source is plentiful.

Therefore, while other migrating birds arrive at the reserve from the north and the northwest to spend the winter, the Indian birds are already beginning to reproduce. Here, the body of water is vast and deep, and it contains fifty species of fish and amphibians. The number of these fish and amphibians must be high, judging by the number of cormorants, snakebirds, and other fish-eating birds that gather in the area.

In November, the reserve becomes the stage for an unusual spectacle. The well-flooded lagunas, which are shallow bodies of water, become crowded with the arrival of migrating birds from the north. Some even come from distances of up to a thousand miles. While the newly hatched young cry out for food, adult ibises spread out their wings to shield their offspring from the rays of the sun. Right around this time, the Antigone cranes also exhibit their festive mating dances.

The reproductive process ceases completely at the beginning of January, and the migratory birds get ready to leave for their return flights. Until May, the air stays dry, and the rising temperature causes ever greater evaporation. These conditions are favorable for the vultures and the marabou storks, as they easily find abundant food in the shallow puddles and pools of water.

If the vegetation and trees of the Bharatpur refuge were cleared for agricultural purposes, such as in many other areas of the Rajasthan region, the refuge would no longer function as a "valve" for the rain that falls so unevenly during different parts of the year. In fact, as soon as the rain would fall, it would quickly wash off

A male Antigone crane performs a mating dance in the Bharatpur bird sanctuary. The Antigone crane is one of the most admired and respected birds in India. It is commonly found in parks and reserves, as well as in the open countryside near cultivated fields and human habitations.

the land in a destructive way, causing erosion. Moreover, the sun would quickly dry out the moisture in the soil, causing it to crack up into blocks.

By setting Bharatpur aside as a reserve, Prince Kishan Singh protected it from the abuses of land management practices that are common in other parts of India. Today, the sanctuary is a sort of promised land for all aquatic birds.

Indian Marsh Birds

What else can one see in this extraordinary

sanctuary, which is so well suited to the tourist who loves adventure but not danger? Among the most visible birds are the cranes. The Antigone cranes live year-round in this area, while the migrating Siberian crane begins arriving in November.

The Antigone crane is one of the most admired and respected birds in India, perhaps because it is almost always found in pairs and represents an obvious example of faithfulness. It is not necessary to go to Bharatpur to see it, as it is found throughout the open countryside in northern India, wherever water is available.

The mating dance of the Antigone crane, like that of the other cranes, helps keep the couple united, and it is not limited to the mating season. *From top to bottom and from left to right:* The male and female rapidly walk in a circle with their wings spread; then the male makes a series of leaps in front of the female; the birds place themselves side to side, after which both raise their heads and make a characteristic trumpeting sound; then they bow their heads, and they may pick up small objects off the ground to toss in the air when they begin to leap.

A group of aquatic birds in an
Indian marsh. The following birds can
be recognized: several wood storks, with
characteristic red face and pink tail; two
young pelicans, which still have a grayish
colored plumage instead of white; a
white heron with a black beak; a large
white heron with a yellow beak. The
aquatic environments in India are a true
paradise for bird watchers, who can find
large concentrations of numerous species
in many parks and reserves.

An Indian lapwing flies near a brown kite, which raises its wings in defense. This type of behavior is called "mobbing," and it is meant to intimidate or dare the other bird. Both the lapwing and the brown kite are very common in India. They often choose to live even in the center of large cities. The lapwing can be found on lawns of parks and near public fountains. The brown kite can be found almost everywhere, endlessly searching for food scraps. Even though the brown kite is considered a bird of prey, it prefers refuse as its food source.

The Antigone crane is found in northern India and in Indochina. The Siberian crane lives in the cold areas of northern Asia during the nesting period. Its numbers have been estimated at between only five hundred and one thousand pairs. In the autumn, this rare bird migrates south to winter in northern India and in China. Until the end of the 1970s, it used to arrive at Bharatpur regularly. From then on, its presence became irregular, leading to fear for its survival.

The storks should not be confused with the cranes. The storks belong to a completely different order of birds (an order is a grouping of families of animals or plants). Various species are found at Bharatpur. One, the Indian anastomo, is characterized by a unique beak that always shows a large opening even when it is closed. Others include the white-necked stork and the larger and more spectacular black-necked stork. Despite their names, these three birds are not similar. Only one of them, the white-necked stork, is closely related to European storks. A good example of the many-colored wood storks that can be seen at Bharatpur is the Indian painted stork, with pink, white, and black feathers.

A typically Indian threesome of birds in the Bharatpur bird sanctuary: a snakebird drying itself on the highest branch; a little lower down are a collared parakeet and a pygmy cormorant, which is the most widespread cormorant in India. It usually lives in large colonies along riverbanks or in aquatic zones.

Storks have the most numerous nests in the preserve, if one counts only the larger birds. In October, they have nests on almost every acacia tree that grows in the marsh or nearby. The loud and rhythmic call of their young is the dominant sound in all of the wet zone.

Besides the colony of wood storks at Bharatpur, another large colony can be seen at the Delhi zoo. Here, the wood storks live among the trees of a small artificial island. They feed their young and come and go undisturbed. They are often seen flying in formations over the city. This is an example of the unusual compromises between humans and nature that only India seems capable of creating and maintaining.

The Bharatpur reserve also contains such smaller storks as the white ibis and the spoonbill, which feed mostly on small animals they catch in the waters of the marsh. Other interesting aquatic birds there are exotic sultanas (they are also common to other marshy areas of India), jacanas, stilt-plovers, small herons, fish-eating martins, Indian lapwings, ducks, geese, snakebirds, pelicans, and three species of cormorants.

Top: The fishing owl is about the same size as the royal owl, but the fishing owl differs by not having feathers on its lower legs. Its lower legs and claws are particularly adapted for catching fish and shellfish. It also hunts birds, reptiles, and mammals, and it occasionally feeds on dead carcasses.

Right: The crested snake eagle (the crest is not very visible in the picture) hides in the thick forest, particularly near bodies of water. It primarily hunts reptiles and small mammals. Now and then it "patrols" its territory in flight, but usually it remains on a tree branch while it waits for its prey to come into sight.

The snakebird is closely related to the cormorant. It is characterized by a longer, snakelike neck and a pointed beak. It swims partly submerged, with only its long S-shaped neck out of the water. The fishing style of the snakebird is peculiar: it thrusts its neck forward, piercing fish with its beak. Like the cormorants, the snakebirds do not have feathers that shed water. To dry out, they must patiently stand in the sun with their wings spread open.

At one time, snakebirds were widespread across a vast area, extending as far as Turkey. However, the recent unexpected drying of Lake Amik in Turkey led to the disappearance of this bird from the Near East. West of India, it is found only in the marshes of Iraq. The snakebird is one of the most ancient birds on earth today. Fossil remains of it have been found that date back to the Eocene epoch, 60 million years ago.

The richness and the variety of the bird life of Bharatpur is such that a hike along the trails provides one of the most interesting and complete spectacles that a student or admirer of aquatic wildlife could ever hope to see.

Land Birds

In the areas of Bharatpur where the trails lead away from the marshes, the bird life is less abundant, but it is still varied and numerous. Cuckoo pheasants and magpie thrushes can be seen hiding in the brush of the forest. One hears the cries of parrots and starlings along with the song of barbets.

The driest and most open zones are the preferred habitat of the aquatic jays and the stone curlews. Vultures regularly roost on the highest branches of dead trees.

Birds of prey are numerous here. On a large tree a few hundred yards from the sanctuary headquarters, a sea eagle regularly builds its nest. Eagles of the steppes (vast, level, treeless tracts of land) and crested snake eagles are found in most areas. The crested snake eagles are beautiful birds with a brown backside and a reddish brown underside with white spots. Their crests are similar to those of the monkey eagles and other crested eagles of the forest. The crest makes these eagles less noticeable when they roost in the foliage of trees, so they can remain unobserved while they await their prey.

The snakebird hunts fish, frogs, and other animals underwater, using its long neck like a harpoon-launcher. While following its prey, the snakebird moves its neck forward and back, like an athlete balancing a javelin. When it is within range, it suddenly launches its neck forward to pierce the prey. Once the prey is captured, the snakebird returns to land, and, with a rapid movement of its head, it removes the fish from its "harpoon." The bird then seizes the fish in midair with its beak open and swallows it. The snakebird is an able "skin diver" and can also fly at high elevations.

HERBIVORES

A person traveling to India in search of wildlife will certainly not be satisfied to see just the birds of Delhi or the beautiful and interesting colonies at Bharatpur, Sultanpur, or Vedhanthangal. The wildlife lover should plan to make a "photo safari," too. Most probably, this person would want to photograph tigers and panthers, along with deer, antelope, wild boars, elephants, and rhinoceroses.

Herbivores (plant-eaters) are generally more common and easily found than the great predators. Any organized tourist group will be almost certain to encounter some of these vegetarian animals occasionally.

Deer

The first great group of Indian herbivores includes the deer. Typically, deer are boreal animals, meaning that they usually belong to forest regions of the north temperate zone (such as in Europe or North America). There are many species of deer in Europe, northern Asia, and North America, but there are only a few kinds in tropical Asia. In India, one of the most common species is the beautiful barasingha, or marsh deer. This animal lives only on the Indian peninsula. Other Indian species are the chital deer, the sambar deer, the hog deer, and the small muntjac deer.

The males of all these species are characterized by beautiful, branched antlers of bone. These are lost every year and grow back to an even larger and more majestic size. The antlers are used as weapons in the rigorous competition in which the males engage to acquire and hold a harem (groups of females dominated by a male). Outside of the mating season, the males form groups that separate from the females. The females are accompanied by their fawns until the young are able to be independent.

Deer are typically forest animals, even in India. They can more easily evade predators by concealing themselves in the forest. Often, they move about at night. The chital deer generally weighs up to 187 pounds (85 kilograms). Its coat has light spots, and it is the most typical deer of the Indian subcontinent.

The musk deer and the rat deer are different from the sambar and the marsh deer because they do not have antlers. They are also smaller. Although this permits

Opposite page: The chital deer is probably the most typical deer in the Indian subcontinent. Like all other members of the deer family, it usually inhabits forests and is agile and graceful. Despite its physical abilities, deer, along with wild boar, are commonly preyed upon by tigers.

Sambar deer are large animals with strong muscles. Males can reach a length of close to 8 feet (2.4 m) and a height of about 4 feet (1.3 m) at the base of the neck. They have larger ears and sinuses than the other deer. Their horns can exceed 3 feet (1 m) in length, but generally they have no more than three points. Sambar deer have a uniformly brown coat that is darker in the males and faded in the females.

them to hide easily, it also means that they are more vulnerable to being preyed upon, even by a wildcat or a large mongoose.

Of the two species, the musk deer is larger and better known. It has two large canine teeth that it uses to defend itself. It also has an unusual musk gland hidden in the skin of the area between its hind legs. This gland emits a fluid that has a strong and disagreeable odor, but, when diluted, it is used as a valuable commercial product in the manufacture of perfumes.

The rat deer is only 10 to 12 inches (25 to 30 cm) tall from the ground to the base of the neck, and it has very short and thin legs. It looks more like an agouti or a small wild pig rather than a hoofed ruminant. (Ruminants are mammals such as sheep, cattle, and deer that, after swallowing food, throw it up, partially digested for final chewing.) Despite its name, this animal is actually not a deer at all. It has many body features that are different from the deer and all other ruminant animals (for example, it does not have antlers).

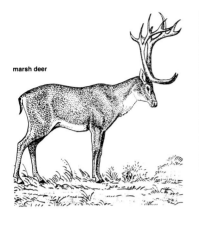
marsh deer

musk deer

rat deer

four-horned antelope

gazelle

Indian Antelope

Various species of antelope also live in India. Unlike deer, these animals typically occupy open areas or areas with a sparse number of trees. Antelope characteristic of India are not found in any other part of the world. This is not true of the tiger and the elephant which, although also characteristic of India, can be found elsewhere.

The largest and the strangest of the antelopes is the nilgau antelope. Its size is close to that of a horse, while its weight is greater. The adult males have a gray, black, and white coat of hair. The females and the young are reddish yellow and brown. This antelope is closely related to three types of African antelope, including the kudu. Genetically, the family of the nilgau antelope occupies a position close to that of the buffalo and oxen.

The nilgau antelope live in groups of four to ten and sometimes even of twenty or more. They occupy the savannas (grasslands) or areas of dry brush, which used to be the preferred habitats of the Asian lion. They graze primarily on the leaves of bushes and the lower leaves of trees, sometimes standing on their hind legs to reach the higher branches.

During periods of dryness, they can survive for a long time without water. The males form groups separate from the females. The males also have the habit of defecating in the center of their territory. Perhaps the odor of their dung acts as a signal of their dominion to possible rivals. Like many other ruminants, the nilgau antelope are polygamous, which means that they mate with more than one female. The males fight intensely among themselves to acquire a harem, although this conflict is usually bloodless and for show only.

During the last decades, the nilgau antelope have greatly increased in number. This is due to the near disappearance of their natural predators (lions are now restricted to the Gir forest, and few tigers remain in the dense forests). The antelope sometimes create problems by damaging farm crops or overgrazing the vegetation in natural environments. This is harmful to other herbivores who depend on this vegetation for food.

The blackbuck antelope is much more agile and quicker than the nilgau. It is a robust animal, weighing almost 90 pounds (40 kg), and its height at the base of the neck is about 2.5 feet (76 cm). At the end of their

Reedbuck antelope roam the vast grasslands of eastern India. These animals spend most of the day in the direct sun. In the hottest hours, they seek out the shade of a few trees.

third year, the males of this species develop a dark, almost black coloring on their backs. This contrasts with the white of their underside, snout, and the area around the eyes. After three years, they also have completely grown their beautiful spiral horns. These sometimes reach a length of over 20 inches (50 cm). With rare exceptions, only males grow horns.

The blackbuck lives in groups and is primarily found on the open plains. It typically lives in arid areas, and it can survive for long periods of time without water. Surprisingly, it withstands direct exposure to the hot rays of the sun in northwest India. This species retreats into the forest if arid conditions become too severe for it. It browses lower than the nilgau antelope, on grasses and leaves of shrubs. Like the African impalas, the blackbuck reacts to danger by bounding away with amazingly high leaps. The leaps of one evidently act as

In the event of danger, reedbuck antelope leap with great agility. Their leaps can sometimes be 18 feet (6 m) long and 9 feet (3 m) high. No carnivores are able to catch them when they begin to leap. Tigers and leopards must use surprise to capture them.

an alarm for the rest of the herd and usually discourage predators from chasing.

Like the nilgau, the reedbuck antelope also practices polygamy, and each year the males that wish to dominate a harem must engage in long, ritualized duels. The reedbuck antelope was overhunted until a few decades ago and was in serious danger of extinction. However, now, thanks to the establishment of parks and preserves and other conservationist measures, the threat has passed. A herd of them was transferred to the state of Texas, where they now have reached five thousand in number.

The third and the last antelope exclusive to India is the small four-horned antelope, the chowsingha. It measures about 24 inches (60 cm) in height at the base of the neck, and it is the only ruminant whose males have four horns. Two of the horns are in the usual position, and the other two are just above the eye sockets.

The chowsingha antelope lives in areas with open vegetation. But, unlike the blackbuck and the nilgau, it cannot survive for long periods without water. It is considered a true antelope of the forest and not of the arid savanna or the desert. The chowsingha is widely hunted, especially by Muslims. The religion of these people forbids them to eat pork, such as the meat of the

43

A herd of domestic buffalo in a marsh in northern India, tended by a herdsman. Water is a necessary element for these large ruminants. They are able to cool and rid themselves of parasites by wading. They feed on marsh plants, roots, rushes, and reeds. Often, their skin becomes covered by mud while they are in water. After the buffalo leave the water, the mud dries and falls off, taking with it the numerous insects that had been nesting in the buffalo's hair.

wild boar

rat deer

four-horned antelope

spotted deer

gaur

Asian buffalo

nilgau antelope

sambar deer

muntjac deer

one-horned rhinoceros

deserts and steppes

savanna with trees

jungle

river environment

46

wild boar. However, they are not forbidden to eat the meat of cows and other similar animals (as the Hindus are). As a result, the four-horned chowsingha antelope has been greatly reduced in number today and is in need of protection. Otherwise, there is danger of losing a unique animal from the Indian fauna.

Animals of the Forests and Swamps

In the jungles of the eastern region of India exist several kinds of large ruminants, closely related to domestic cattle and to the extinct aurochs of the European forests. The largest and the most extraordinary of the animals in this family is the gaur.

This magnificent animal is normally about 6 feet (2 m) tall at the base of the neck, and it can exceed one ton in weight. It is black, except for the lower parts of the legs, which are white. It has an impressive hump similar to that of the bison and large horns that curve inward. The horns reach over 2 feet (61 cm) in length, and these deadly weapons protect the gaur from the attacks of any type of predator.

The gaur is found primarily in hilly forests. It feeds mostly on grasses, calmly grazing in clearings. Gaurs live in small groups, with the males separated from the females and their young. During the mating season, which normally lasts from November to March, the males engage in violent duels to win the females. On these occasions, it is possible to hear their loud calls from a distance of more than half a mile (1 km).

The gestation, or pregnancy, usually lasts nine months, and the young are generally born one at a time. They are nursed for a period of almost nine months. At the age of two to three years, the young calves reach maturity. At this time, they are ready to enter the group of other members that have the ability to reproduce.

The wild buffalo are about the same size as the gaur, but they have much larger horns. In some cases, they reach up to 6 feet (2 m) in length. They differ from the common domestic buffalo in that they have a more slender and powerful appearance.

The buffalo inhabit the forests, and they like to bask in water and mud for many hours of the day. Like the gaur, the buffalo are a tough prey to catch even for a tiger. If they feel threatened, they may even charge a human. When they are about to charge, they raise their

Opposite page: Environmental grouping of the principal Indian ruminant animals. In the Asian region, there are ruminants adapted to every type of environment and vegetation cover. Four-horned antelope and nilgau antelope are found in the driest environments; the wild boar and the deer correspond to the savanna environments, although they prefer forest areas; the gaur, muntjac deer, and the rat deer prefer forest environments, too. The Asian buffalo and the one-horned rhinoceros are typically associated with river and marsh environments, where they spend much of their time in the mud.

47

A one-horned rhinoceros (with a heron on its back) in the wetlands of the Kaziranga reserve, in the Indian state of Assam. The majority of the surviving one-horned rhinoceroses live in India. More than half of the entire world population (400 out of 740, according to a 1966 census) is concentrated in the Kaziranga reserve. A few still live in Nepal.

snout and let out a typical grunt, sometimes stamping their front hooves on the ground. The domestic buffalo, which are widespread around the world, are calmer than the wild buffalo.

The Indian Rhinoceros

A large size and powerful horns can provide a herbivore with an effective alternative to fleeing when facing a predator. This evolutionary path has been taken not only by the gaur and the buffalo but, to a certain extent, by some other herbivores as well. These herbivores range from the nilgau antelope to the gigantic Indian elephant and include, particularly, the rhinoceros. The rhinoceros is perhaps the most characteristic of the animals that have evolved in this direction.

In India, of the three original Asian species of rhinoceros, only the one-horned Indian rhinoceros has survived. It is the largest, reaching almost 6 feet (2 m) in height and weighing up to two tons.

The three Asian rhinoceroses are thought to be in danger of extinction, despite an increase in the populations of the one-horned Indian rhinoceros and the Java rhinoceros. The rhinoceros has had the same physical features for at least a million years. The diagram shows the populations according to 1970 and 1983 estimates (each box equals 100 rhinoceroses).

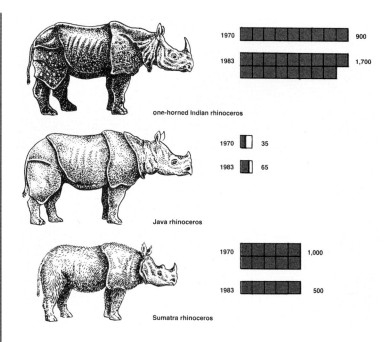

one-horned Indian rhinoceros

1970		900
1983		1,700

Java rhinoceros

1970		35
1983		65

Sumatra rhinoceros

1970		1,000
1983		500

Although armored like creatures of former ages, the Indian rhinoceroses are peaceful animals that like to wallow in swamps that form when the plain of the Ganges River becomes flooded. They are usually thought of as solitary animals. Actually, when visiting their proper habitat, one can find several of them in close association.

There is a serious threat to rhinoceroses that arises from poaching. These extraordinary animals are in danger of extinction because of their value to humans. These animals are representatives of an ancient age when humans had not yet played a dominant role. In a certain sense, it is ironic that at a time approaching the twenty-first century after landings have been made on the moon, the fate of these unique mammals could be so heavily valued for their medicinal and magical powers from beliefs that date back to the Middle Ages.

THE ASIAN ELEPHANT

Among the giant Asian herbivores that have been threatened by extinction or reduced in number and area, there is one that has successfully endured modern influences. Its numbers are still high, not only in its native forests but also in the domestic state, as a collaborator with humans. This animal is the most gigantic of all the herbivores — the elephant.

Problems of a Gigantic Animal

The Asian elephant is about 10 feet (3 m) tall at the shoulder and weighs from 6,600 to 8,800 pounds (3,000 to 4,000 kg). It is the largest terrestrial animal in Asia and the second largest animal in the world. Only the African elephant is larger, reaching 11 feet (3.5 m) in height and weighing from 13,200 to 15,400 pounds (6,000 to 7,000 kg).

Although it is similar to the African elephant in shape, the Asian elephant is easily identified by a less wrinkled trunk that has only one fingerlike appendage at its top. The Asian elephant also has a strongly convex and bilobed (divided into two lobes) forehead region. Its ears are smaller and less rounded than those of the African elephant. Furthermore, its tusks are not as large. The heaviest Asian elephant tusks weigh 154 pounds (70 kg), while those of the African elephant can weigh up to 300 pounds (136 kg). There is also a difference in the design on the crown of the molar teeth.

The African elephant typically lives in the savannas, but the Asian elephant prefers the forests. Besides a general physical similarity, these two animals also have a similar and unusual social organization of their herds.

Despite their appearance, these animals are not as ancient as one might believe. In their present form, they originated at about the same time as humans, three to four million years ago. Their ancestors originated however, about forty million years ago. The remains of one of these early animals (Moeritherium) was discovered in a marsh on the banks of the Nile River in Africa. It did not have a trunk or tusks, and it was no larger than a hog. It probably lived in the water like a hippopotamus.

Trunked animals evolved into larger animals and, because of this, problems of movement and support of the body weight had to be solved. Despite their huge appearance, the limbs of the elephant are perfected

Opposite page: A magnificent male Indian elephant with fully developed tusks. Elephant tusks are actually upper incisor teeth that have been transformed in a very particular way. One-third of the tusk is embedded in the tooth socket, and one-sixth of it is covered by the gums. Only half of the tusk remains outside of the elephant's mouth. The tusk is more or less curved upward. There is no enamel on the tusk surface, except for a small zone near the tip that is quickly worn away.

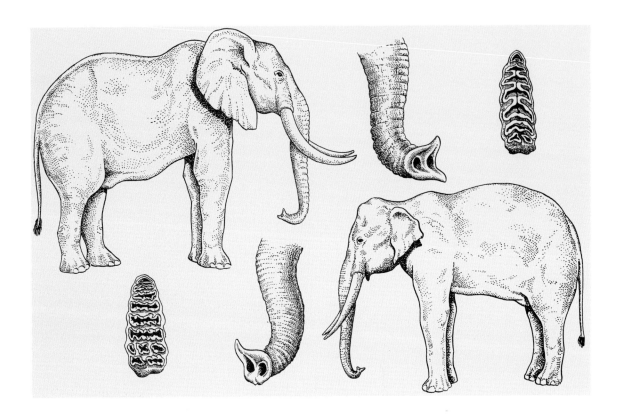

Illustration of the principal differences between the African elephant (*top left*) and the Indian elephant (*bottom right*). The African elephant is much larger, sometimes reaching 11 feet (3.5 m) in height at the base of the neck and weighing 7 tons. The Indian elephant does not exceed 9.5 feet (3 m) and weighs 3 to 4 tons. The tusks of the Indian elephant are shorter and lighter than those of the African elephant. The crowns of their molar teeth have a different design, resulting from the consumption of different foods. The trunk is not as wrinkled and has one fingerlike appendage near the top. While the African elephant typically lives in the savanna, the Indian elephant is perfectly adapted to life in the forest.

structures. The five toes are enclosed within a fibrous, fatty tissue, and they form a flat and wide surface that keeps the elephant from sinking into soft ground. The toes also have independent bones that give the elephant great sensitivity in walking.

The elephant's typical movement is the so-called amble. The two feet on one side are moved forward at the same time, alternating with the two feet on the other side. The majority of other four-footed animals, or quadrupeds, instead first move the front-right foot and the back-left foot, and then the front-left and the back-right feet.

In order to chew the necessary enormous quantity of food, about 500 to 600 pounds (227 to 272 kg) per day, the elephants have very specialized molar teeth. There are three for every half jaw, but they are not all used at the same time. The part of each group of teeth closest to the outside of the mouth is used first. After several years when these areas are worn out, the teeth that are farther back inside the mouth are used. This horizontal direction continues until the third molars are

A fire is set in the forest to clear new land for farming. The continual clearing of forests for farms and human settlements has greatly reduced the space available to elephants and all other large Indian animals. These animals have become more and more restricted to the protected parks and reserves. Sometimes there can be too great a concentration of large animals in these protected areas, which leads to a scarcity of food. When this occurs, the animals may stray outside the limits of the reserves in search of food. This creates problems for both humans and elephants.

used up, and the health of the old, toothless elephant gradually deteriorates until it dies.

What distinguishes the elephant the most from all other animals is the trunk. The trunk gives the elephant extraordinary capabilities. It can be used to pick up both large and small objects. It can drive away a possible enemy, and it can evaluate the quality of available food. It is really a very special kind of hand, having a sense of touch, smell, and taste. With such a remarkably efficient appendage, the elephant was able to develop a system of social relations beyond the lower level of the hippopotamuses and the rhinoceroses.

Social Organization

The social organization of elephants is essentially based on the "matriarchal group," composed of females and young males below the age of sexual maturity (ten to thirteen years of age). Adult males are limited to following the females from a distance, waiting for the rare moment when the female has an impulse to mate. Mating occurs every four years, gestation lasts twenty months, and the young is nursed for about two years.

These Indian elephants are equipped for transporting tourists. The domestication and training of the Indian elephant is an ancient practice. Herodotus (fifth century B.C. Greek historian) wrote of having seen them walking in the streets of Babylon, unloading ships in the ports, and transporting equipment and soldiers. As long as 2,500 years ago, this elephant was exported from India to Mesopotamia (Iraq, today). It may have been living wild in that area, too, if one accepts the inscriptions of King Assur-nasir-pal, which recorded the killing of thirty elephants on one of his hunting trips in 850 B.C. Almost 1,000 years before this time, the Egyptian pharoah Tutmasi III, conqueror of Asia Minor, was said to have killed two hundred elephants at one time. It is not surprising that the Asian elephant has disappeared from Asia Minor after such massacres as these.

When a female begins to show her readiness for mating, the various eager males confront each other and enter into a state of "fury." They become irritable and upset. They trumpet in a characteristic way, and the glands near their temples increase in size.

Taming Elephants

Today, Asian elephants live in a wild state only in a few areas of the Indian subcontinent, Indochina, Sumatra, and northern Borneo. In the past, they were also found in China, Pakistan, Afghanistan, Iran, Iraq, and Turkey. Ancient documents confirm the existence in these areas of a forgotten "elephant culture."

Between the Tigris and Euphrates rivers (what is now the country of Iraq) in 850 B.C., the Assyrian king Assur-nasir-pal killed thirty elephants in one hunt. He ordered that his feat be recorded in an inscription. The kind of elephants that lived between these two rivers is probably the kind that Pyrrhus used in Italy when his army attacked the empire of Rome in 281 B.C. It was also the same kind the Syrian king Antiochus III used to fight against Egypt in 217 B.C.

With the passing of time and the spread of the Asian deserts due to deforestation by humans, the environment in western Asia was deeply changed. The pachyderms — the elephant, the rhino, and the hippo — were not able to adapt to these environments.

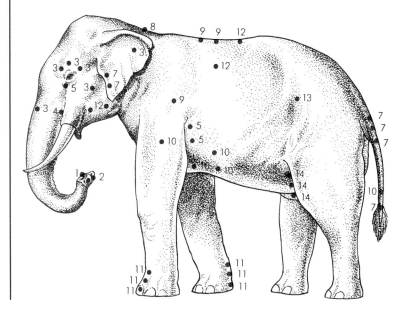

By stimulating certain nerve center points, called nila, the elephant driver (mahout) is able to get the elephant to respond in certain ways. Several of these points are illustrated here, with the explanation of the elephant's response: (1) rolls up the trunk; (2) extends the trunk; (3) returns to the control of the driver; (4) walks backwards; (5) kneels; (6) offers its shoulders so the driver can mount; (7) walks; (8) lowers the head; (9) stops; (10) stops; (11) lifts the front leg so the driver can mount; (12) offers the saddle to the driver; (13) stops and keeps the trunk drooping; (14) moves in a circle.

Asian elephant works in Malaysia. Asian elephants have lived together with humans for thousands of years, even though they have always maintained a certain independence and personality not unlike horses. "Character" varies from animal to animal, and their ability to understand human language is incredible. They have a complex social organization. For example, the females help each other during the birth of offspring, and older animals that have lost their group may be temporarily admitted into another group.

Elephants have distinct personalities. Like humans, they are subject to complex emotions. They have a trusting and cooperative relationship with their trainers. This trust is repaid by the trainer, who cares for the elephant by making sure it is not overworked. The trainer brings the animal to be bathed at the end of each workday. The animal is cooled off, and its parasites are removed.

The domestication of elephants is an ancient art. In the Assam region of India, a document (the Hastividyarnava) written in the local language explains in detail all the techniques for capturing and training elephants. Entire herds were driven into large wooden pens and then immobilized with the help of trained elephants. Each newly captured elephant was entrusted to a cornak, an elephant tamer. With extraordinary patience, the trainer calmed the elephant and, little by little, taught it to respond to a considerable number of commands. Some of these were: forward, back, stop, raise the foot, raise the trunk, go into the water, push with the foot or with the head, and knock down an obstacle.

This process could require years for completion. Once trained, however, elephants could perform various kinds of work. The best trained animals worked with few orders. They completed complicated work projects with a great sense of initiative and cooperation with a crew.

In Sri Lanka, at Kegalle, there is a training center that rents elephants out for farm work. The work schedule is from 7:00 A.M. until 2:00 P.M. Elephants are

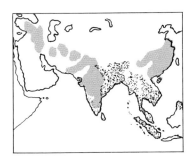

Past territory (colored zone) and present territory (dotted zone) of the Asian elephant. Unlike the African elephant, which lives in the savanna and eats bark and dried shrubs, the Asian elephant prefers humid forest zones. The Asian elephant is characterized by a less adaptable temperature-regulating system and diet. For these reasons, it has disappeared from the Middle Eastern and Chinese regions, as the jungle was converted to farming. This elephant lives only in India and Southeast Asia, where there are ample areas of thick vegetation.

often used to transport trunks of valuable lumber trees in parts of the jungle where vehicles are unable to penetrate. The trainer makes sure that the load is not too heavy and that the animal receives the proper amount of food. Then, at the end of the workday, the cornak brings the elephant to a body of water where it cools off. Here, the trainer removes the parasites that have attached themselves to the elephant's skin.

The Sri Lankan trainers often guide the elephants without calling out orders. They do this by pressing their heels against special sensitive areas of the elephant that are called "nila." Many of these areas correspond to special groups of nerve cells, or ganglions. Other areas seem to correspond to the Chinese acupuncture points.

A Sri Lankan scholar named Paul Deraniyagala spent many years identifying these nerve centers. He discovered at least ninety of them. According to him, nerve centers of the African elephants had to have been known in the past, since the Carthaginian general Hannibal used domesticated African elephants in his attack on Rome in 218 B.C. Unfortunately, with the destruction of Carthage, this knowledge was lost. This would account for the fact that up until now it has not been possible to domesticate the African elephant the way the Carthaginians once did, more than two thousand years ago.

In Sri Lanka, knowledge of elephant nerve centers also goes back to ancient times. At the World Congress on Acupuncture held in Paris in 1979, Professor A. Jayasuriya (president of the Sri Lanka Acupuncture Society), presented a thousand-year-old document written on palm leaves. The writings contained instructions for using acupuncture on elephants. According to Deraniyagala, in the past in Sri Lanka, life-sized brass models of elephants were constructed. The nerve centers were then marked by red points. Inside the brass elephant, a complicated device was placed that would move the elephant-robot in a manner similar to that of a real elephant when one of the nerve points was touched.

These expensive elephant-robots served to educate the nobility (who owned the animals) as to how to control live elephants. This was important because the elephant was useful in war.

MONKEYS

The tropical jungle is a tangle of plants and trees full of the sounds of the animals that inhabit it. One hears cries, howls, calls, the rustling of branches and twigs, and the trampling of leaves. These are the sounds documentary and adventure films present. They are also the sounds announcing the approach of a group of monkeys.

In India, with the exception of one humanlike ape (the ulock, which is limited to a few eastern zones of India and Indochina), all other monkeys can be grouped in two subfamilies. One subfamily includes the macaco monkeys. The other includes the colobin and the langur monkeys. The first group spends less time in trees and is primarily omnivorous (eating both plants and animals). The second group is arboreal (living in trees) and strictly vegetarian.

The most common and familiar of the groups are the rhesus monkeys from the first group and the langur monkeys from the second. Both kinds are common in India. They sometimes venture into zones that are inhabited by humans to seek food scraps. Occasionally, they can even be seen near temples, markets, and railway stations.

Langurs

The langur monkeys are considered sacred animals by the followers of the Hindu religion. For this reason, they are rarely bothered, at least near areas where Hindus live. The situation can be different in the forests, since several tribes of jungle nomads regard any animal as a possible food source.

In some areas, it is easy to find a group of langur monkeys in the forest. One need only walk for some time in a quiet area or move slowly by car on a road that cuts through the territory of these monkeys. Their presence is immediately signaled by incredible sights and sounds of the movement of leaves and the bending and breaking of twigs and bushes. For someone who is accustomed to thinking of monkeys as tree-swinging acrobats, this experience can be upsetting. It is hard to imagine that these little "imps of the woods" could cause such a disturbance in their habitat.

When a langur or macaco monkey is alarmed, its first reaction is to jump down from the tree and run away on the ground. This behavior is different from that

Opposite page: Next to the rhesus monkey, which is found almost everywhere, the capped cacaco is the most common monkey in Asia. Unlike the rhesus monkey, the capped macaco lives primarily in forests and does not have a close association with humans. It is more agile than the rhesus monkey, and it has a characteristic tuft of hair on its head.

of the gibbons, which flee from branch to branch, hanging by their hands.

The worst enemy of the langur monkey is the leopard. If a langur monkey sees a leopard or a tiger or any other animal that arouses suspicion, it makes a throaty signal to warn the entire group. The gleeful sound langur monkeys make when they hop from tree to tree, or when they are occupied with pleasant activities, is much different from the alarm sound.

The langur monkey reaches a length of up to 2.5 feet (76 cm) and has a tail over 3 feet (100 cm) long. This long tail has served to favor its evolution as a tree-dwelling, or arboreal, animal. A langur weighs between 19 and 35 pounds (9 and 16 kg), and this easily explains the extreme disturbance of the leaves and brush that is caused when it moves.

The coat of hair has a light color, nearly silver or golden-gray. This coloring depends on the light under which langurs are seen, and it varies from place to place. The face, ears, and the feet are black in color.

Langur monkeys are strictly vegetarian, and they

The langur is a robust tree monkey that is strictly vegetarian. It lives in well-organized social groups that are not rigidly ranked. Langurs do not exhibit aggressive behavior, nor do they have defensive tactics. They prefer to flee when an enemy is encountered. The langur monkey is not afraid of humans. In fact, it often comes near human habitations and sometimes raids gardens and orchards.

live in well-organized social groups. These groups have a weak ranking system, or hierarchy, in comparison to the social systems of other monkeys. A group of fifteen to twenty-five animals can occupy a territory ranging from 0.39 to 5 sq. miles (1 to 13 sq. km). The langur monkeys tend to expand their territory in areas that are very dry.

Their necessary resources are water, leaves, and trees for sleeping. Since these resources are so plentiful, the langur monkeys are not inclined to fight over them. This explains why there is little ranking within groups and little hostility between different groups of langur monkeys. In short, the langur monkeys are arboreal animals that live in ideal conditions of peace and abundance.

Males do not even fight over females, according to scientists who have observed groups of langur monkeys in the mating period. Except in the case of a dominant male, there is no correlation between the social rank of a langur monkey and the number of matings it has. There are no fixed mating pairs or harems. The mating system seems to be based on the availability of partners.

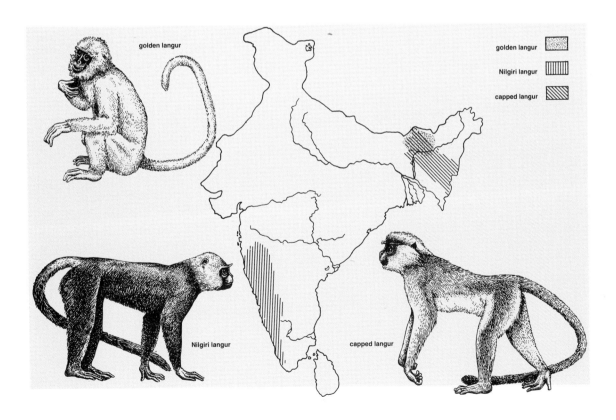

golden langur

golden langur

Nilgiri langur

capped langur

Nilgiri langur

capped langur

This illustration shows a group of resting macacos. The strict ranking system of the macacos can be seen in the formation made by different groups in the course of their activities. When the macacos are resting, as in this case, the center of the group is occupied by dominant males and females with their very young offspring. Meanwhile, the young macacos and the "subleaders" form a defensive ring around this inner group. While walking, the first group remains in the center, as the second group occupies the front and rear positions.

As soon as an offspring is born, the mother is put outside the social system. This does not bother her. Her only concern is that the offspring remains within the social system. She does not become involved in disputes related to dominance or subordination. The other monkeys of her group respect her maternity. They do not bother her, unless they seek to "borrow" the little one for a short time. The mother readily consents to this, although she constantly keeps an eye on the young langur and grabs it back at the first sign of restlessness. The young langur monkey recognizes its mother from the very first days of its life. It holds out its arms to her as soon as she comes near.

The young monkey is weaned toward the fifteenth month. Sexual maturity is reached after the third year. Gestation lasts six months, and a female can give birth every two years.

There are three other species of monkeys in India that are related to the langur. They all live in a manner similar to that of the langur, except that they do not go near human habitations, and they always hide themselves in the dense forest.

One of these monkeys is the Nilgiri langur. Unfortunately, the Nilgiri langur is in danger of extinction because, for many years, it has been widely hunted for its beautiful fur. Also, some people claim that its meat, blood, and various organs have medicinal value. Because of this, the monkey has become rare today, and it will not permit humans to come near it.

A capped macaco perches on a liana vine. Most of the macaco species live in Asia, from the Indian region to Japan and Indonesia. They are all strongly social and strictly ranked. Their adaptability to the changes caused by humans varies according to the different species. The rhesus monkey has adapted well, but the lionine monkey is in serious danger of extinction.

Macacos

The life of the rhesus macaco is much different from that of the langur. The macaco monkeys are reddish yellow with a pink face and a short tail. They spend more time on the ground than the langurs. They also have a more rigid system of social ranking. Each group of these monkeys has a leader and several other higher-ranking members that are referred to as an "aristocracy." Their social system is determined by intense fighting, which occurs each time a new monkey enters the group.

According to the majority of scientists that study monkeys, this behavior is necessary when a species "comes down from the trees" and begins to live

65

Two rhesus monkeys (one young and one adult) rest on the walls of a temple. These animals fearlessly approach homes and public buildings throughout India. The unknowing visitor mistakes these animals for pets when this happens. In the city, the rhesus monkey eats all types of refuse, and it often begs for food from travelers in airports and railway stations.

primarily on the ground. This also occurred with the baboons of eastern Africa, the barbary ape of Morocco and Algeria, and the macacos of Japan.

Like the other monkeys and apes that have left their original habitats, the macacos have also stopped being strictly vegetarian. They now are omnivorous, eating insects, spiders, and sometimes even lizards, frogs, and bird eggs. They also eat fruit, leaves, and vegetables, and they will sometimes raid gardens and cultivated fields to get this food. They can be seen in groups in public parks, near temples, and in railroad stations begging for food from people. Rhesus monkeys are commonly seen near the University of Delhi. One sometimes hears reports of their biting people.

Despite these infrequent inconveniences, the monkeys generally live in peaceful harmony in areas of human habitation. Monkeys can be found in many temples and public places in the city, and they are well behaved and friendly. It is not unusual to see them on the buildings at the Delhi airport, ready to run toward someone who seems willing to give them a scrap of food. However, the monkeys occasionally pay a price for this familiarity with humans. Although the majority of people do not disturb the rhesus monkeys, sometimes people capture a large number of them to be sold and exported as experimental animals. This is a sad and unfortunate fate for these animals that are so intelligent, social, and trusting of humans.

The scientific interest in the rhesus monkey comes from the animal's strong similarities with humans. They are much closer to humans than rats, guinea pigs, dogs, or cats. Also, rhesus monkeys are easy to keep in captivity. Besides the humanitarian aspect, the exportation of large numbers of rhesus macacos has caused occasional decreases in their populations. It was fortunate that the Indian government now imposes strict limitations on exports.

Among the other species of macacos present in India is the white-bearded macaco. This monkey is very different from the other macacos. It is covered by a thick, almost black fur, and its face is framed by a unique silver-colored mane of hair. The end of its tail is tufted like the lion's tail.

CARNIVORES

Many predatory mammals hide and move around in the tall grasses and the dense jungles, hunting both small and large animals with every kind of technique. Despite the dense human population of the Indian subcontinent, several of these carnivores (meat-eaters) are still common and widespread. Their presence continues to give the Indian jungle the typical atmosphere that excites all of those who read the stories of Rudyard Kipling.

The Leopard

The leopard can be found throughout most of India. There are two kinds of leopards. One is spotted, and the other is of a dark color and is commonly known as the black panther. In Kipling's *The Jungle Book*, the faithful friend of Mowgli was a black panther named Bagheera.

Black panthers and leopards are different-colored versions of the same species, like blonds and brunettes among humans. By closely observing the coat of a black panther, one can notice the design of spots that stands out against the background of a different tone of black. Scientific studies have shown that the gene for a black coat is recessive. This means that if a spotted leopard mates with a black panther, the first generation of offspring will all be spotted. This explains why the black panther is rarer than the spotted leopard everywhere leopards are found.

Compared with the tiger, the leopard is often considered a relatively small animal that is not especially dangerous. However, it can reach a length of 7 feet (215 cm) and a weight of 110 to 120 pounds (50 to 55 kg). It is capable of hunting not only large rodents, monkeys, reptiles, and birds, but also small deer, domestic animals, dogs, and, in some cases, humans.

The leopard is not as closely associated with the forest as the tiger. In India, it can be found in relatively open areas and even near villages, provided the terrain is somewhat rocky and there is some vegetation. Among the most common prey of these "suburban" leopards are stray dogs, which are found almost everywhere.

"The leopard," writes Pierre Pfeffer, "does not hesitate to enter a house while chasing a dog. A large dog that had the habit of following me, usually slept on the porch of my hut in the forest. However, one night it came into my bedroom and hid under my bed,

Opposite page: The Temminck cat (golden cat) is one of the "minor" wildcats of the Indian jungle. It is especially widespread in the Himalayas. It is no larger than a lynx, but it is believed to prey on such ruminant animals as small goats or deer fawns.

The Asian lion was once widespread from the Mediterranean basin to northern India. Today, it survives in a limited number that is found only in the reserve of the Gir forest. Even in the reserve, its existence is threatened by a difficult coexistence with people. Some people consider the lion a constant menace to livestock, and they continue to kill it whenever it is found.

whimpering in fear. I grabbed my flashlight and went outside, and I noticed the phosphorescent reflection of the eyes of a leopard that was not more than 50 steps from the hut. It was evident that the leopard would have chased the dog if it had not heard the sound of my voice."

The Asian Lion

Even the rare Asian lion is not exclusively a forest carnivore. The nearly two hundred survivors of this magnificent species live today exclusively in the Gir forest of northwestern India. This jungle is composed of teak, palas, jambul, and ber trees, along with short bamboo and an underbrush of more or less prickly bushes.

In the past, Asian lions lived more toward the west, extending as far as Turkey, Palestine, and even south-eastern Europe. The Greek historian Herodotus wrote

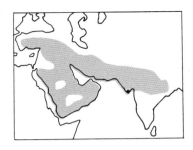

The shaded area shows the past territory of the Asian lion. Today, this animal has almost completely disappeared from its former vast area of distribution. The lion was present even on the European continent until the fifth century B.C., according to the writings of the Greek historian Herodotus.

about them in the fifth century B.C. The lion was the subject of many ancient works of art and sculpture created in the areas now occupied by Egypt, Israel, Iran, Iraq, Greece, and Italy.

Little by little, lions were exterminated in every corner of their vast area of distribution, except for Africa and the remote forest of the Gir wildlife preserve. The remaining lions at Gir feed on wild boar and several kinds of antelope and deer. Occasionally, when these animals are scarce, the lion may resort to preying on the domestic animals of the area's farmers.

The results of this can be disastrous. In the past, the farmers of the Gir area often used poison to prevent lions from preying on their animals. The Gir lions have always been harmless in regard to humans. In fact, people have been known to come close to them, while the lions are stopped on a well-traveled trail, without harm.

Today, the Asian lion is listed in the "red book" of animals in danger of extinction. The lion is the subject of careful measures on the part of the Indian government aimed at safeguarding it. There are also several local organizations working to protect this animal. They are trying to convince the shepherd-farmers to move their herds elsewhere. This would keep the lions from being poisoned, and it would stop the livestock's overgrazing that damages the forests. Unfortunately, in India there is not an abundance of alternative areas.

The problems associated with humans living in harmony with these large animals are delicate. At Gir, the accepted habit of using young buffalo as bait to attract lions so that they can be photographed by tourists has certainly not helped the lions readapt to hunting on their own.

Cats and Small Carnivores of the Jungle

Many kinds of cats can be found in the Indian jungle. In addition to large cats such as the tiger, the lion, and the leopard, there are at least five other species of smaller cats from this same genus or grouping of related species. The nebulous leopard is found in the eastern regions (Nepal, Bhutan, Sikkim). It is the largest and the most mysterious of the smaller species. It is a little over 6 feet (2 m) long, including the tail, and weighs from 40 to 44 pounds (18 to 20 kg). The smaller cats include the marbled cat, which is smaller than the nebulous cat; the

This illustration shows the division of the various wild cats into different habitats in the Indian region. *From left to right:* the leopard (on the tree branch) and the tiger, forest dwellers; the leopard (in the foreground) inhabits areas with a more sparse vegetation, such as savannas or secondary forests. The lion, which now is found only in the Gir Reserve, is strictly a savanna predator. A hunting female is shown in the center of the illustration along with an adult male. The snow leopard inhabits the inaccessible mountain habitats at high elevations.

Temmick cat, which is similar to a miniature puma; the Bengala cat, the fishing cat, the jungle cat, and the Sri Lankan cat.

Besides these forest cats, there are other cats in India that live in the open and rocky zones. These include the Pallas cat (which has a plump appearance, small ears, and characteristic marks on the snout), the North African wildcat, the desert lynx, and the lynx of the north temperate zones. Of these last three animals, the wildcat and the desert lynx are the most common in the arid zones of northwest India. The lynx of the north temperate zone lives in areas near the Himalayas. There it finds a climate similar to that of Siberia and northern Europe, where this species is particularly widespread.

All the cats mentioned in this section are nocturnal, and they often travel from tree to tree through the forest. For this reason, they are hard to observe and study. They feed on rodents, birds, insects, reptiles, amphibians, and

fish. The fishing cat is specialized in capturing fish, and it enters the water up to its belly to grab them.

The civets are carnivores that should not be confused with the other cats. Generally, the civets are longer and have noses that are more pointed. They are as agile as the cats, and, at times, they are just as cautious and mysterious. Two kinds of civets are commonly found in India, and they are not difficult to keep in captivity.

Most civets secrete a white or yellow substance from glands located at the base of the tail. The smell of this fluid is intolerable until it is diluted. In its diluted form, it is useful in the manufacture of perfumes. The natural function of this smelly secretion seems to be that of repelling possible predators.

Other unusual civets live in the far eastern part of the Indian peninsula (Nepal, Sikkim, Bhutan). They are the linsanghi and the binturong civets. They are primarily found in Malaysia and Indochina.

The fur-bearing carnivores are generally found in

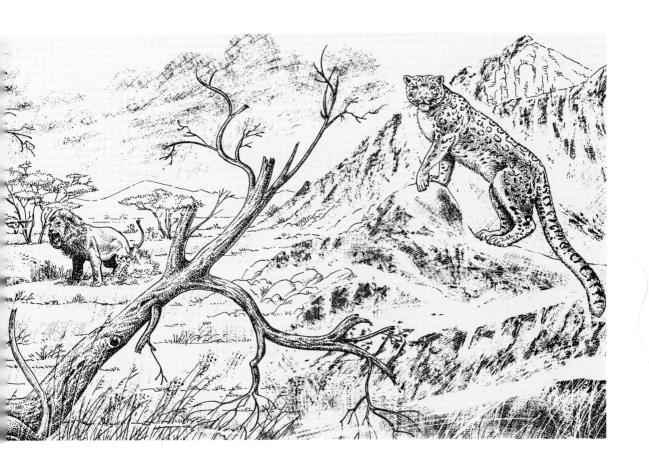

honey-eater

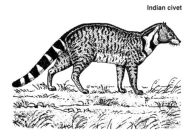

Indian civet

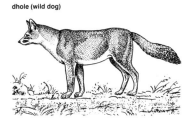

dhole (wild dog)

Tibetan bear

lipped bear

northern India. They include the large ratele, the strange ferret badger, the hog-nose badger, the marten, the weasel, and the otter. Many of these animals inhabit the forests, while the snake-hunting animals, such as the mongooses, inhabit the open and cultivated zones.

However, some species of mongooses inhabit the forests and areas near streams, and they have habits that are similar to those of the otters. These include the large mongoose with the striped neck, which preys on many types of birds, reptiles, and small mammals up to the size of rabbits. The crab-eating mongoose lives farther north and preys primarily on shellfish (crustaceans), fish, and frogs, which it catches in the mountain streams of the Himalayan zone.

Canines and Hyenas

The canine family is well represented in India. The jackal, wolf, fox, small Indian fox, and wild dog are all widespread. The wild dog, or dhole, is one of the most interesting social hunters in the tropical regions. It reaches a total length of over 4 feet (1 m) and weighs from 33 to 44 pounds (15 to 20 kg). The wild dog is smaller than a wolf and has a more reddish color and rounded ears. Its tail is bushier, and it has six molars (the wolf has seven) in the lower jaw.

Like the wolf and the African hunting dog, the dhole is a capable group hunter. Many legends and stories have arisen from this ability. The most common prey of the dhole are wild boars and deer. Some people in India say that they even attack buffalo, bears, and tigers. Generally, dholes hide in the forest, where they hunt more during the day than at night. In recent years, their population has been greatly reduced and so has their habitat. Many have been killed off by humans, but, thanks to the establishment of numerous parks and wildlife reserves, they are now in no great danger of extinction.

The golden jackal is smaller and more widespread than the dhole. It measures about 3 feet (1 m) and weighs from 17 to 24 pounds (7.7 to 11 kg). These animals generally move about in pairs in every type of environment, including suburban areas.

The wolves of India are slightly smaller than those of America and Eurasia. These are the wolves of the pack of Akela, which helped bring up Mowgli in

Kipling's story. The story might have some basis in reality. In the Indian news, there has been more than one report of children that have been raised by wolves. One example is the famous case of the children Amala and Kamala, who were found near Midnapore in 1920. An occurrence of this type is at least, theoretically, possible, since there is some similarity between the social behaviors of humans and wolves. One must not forget that, today, descendants of the wolf live among humans as pet dogs.

The Lipped Bear

Another animal friend of Mowgli in *The Jungle Book* is Bhalu, the lipped bear. This animal is the smallest and most widespread of the three species of bears found in India. It is almost 6 feet (2 m) long and weighs about 260 pounds (118 kg). Like most of the animals in the bear family, the lipped bear is an omnivore. It feeds mainly on ants, termites, and other small insects.

THE TIGER

Many forests in India and throughout tropical Asia have been set aside as parks or special reserves, and they are crossed by service roads and trails. However, this does not mean that a single, unarmed person can penetrate and wander undisturbed in these forests without experiencing a strong sense of danger. The main source of this danger, has a well-defined identity — the tiger.

Origins of the Tiger

The tiger can be considered the strongest and most powerful and beautiful of all the large carnivores living on the earth. It originated at the beginning of the Pleistocene epoch (two to three million years ago) in the northern part of the Asian continent.

This animal has always remained exclusive to Asia, even after the long migrations that occurred during the glacial period, which ended ten thousand years ago. These migrations moved the tiger south and southwest, toward the luxurious tropical forests of India and Indochina. They also moved it to the west, toward the Caspian Sea and across the Caucasus Mountains to the Black Sea. The widespread presence of the tiger shows that it can exist in almost any area where there are forests or tall grasslands in which to live and hunt. The tiger did not spread into Africa, probably because of the dryness of Asia's southwestern border areas.

The lion, an inhabitant of savannas and arid lands, could live in Africa as well as in Asia and Europe. A small number of lions have survived in India. In the past, the two largest cats of the world lived "next door to each other" in many areas of Asia, without entering into competition with one another. The great cat with the striped coat was actually a predator specialized for the forests, while the reddish yellow hunter was specialized for the savannas.

Habitat and Hunting Techniques

The tiger reached the hot forests of India from its original Siberian forests during a relatively recent period, perhaps some tens of thousands of years ago. For a long time, it lived undisturbed in various environments. The tiger is a solitary animal, though not antisocial. It is territorial like the lion but much more wary and withdrawn.

Opposite page: A striking example of a tiger emerges from thick vegetation. This animal symbolizes Indian wildlife more than any other animal. The tiger originated in the Siberian forests, where only several hundred tigers survive today. In the course of its expansion to other areas, it became adapted to the hot Indo-Malaysian forests. The vast western Asian deserts formed a barrier to the tiger's expansion of territory.

The tiger is well adapted to moving through dense vegetation and adopting either a motionless or a moving ambush. In the shadows and light of the jungle, the striped coat of the tiger is almost invisible. A motionless tiger in ambush can remain this way for many minutes without being noticed by either humans or animals. It either remains hidden among the vegetation while waiting for its prey (most often a deer or a wild boar), or it follows prey. Stories have been told of persons being followed at a distance by the great hunter that never came near or came out into the open. In most cases, these people were not attacked by the great cat. Some people say the animal's behavior was due to its curiosity. More probably, the behavior came from an inner conflict between the desire to capture a prey and the fear of humans.

Although the Indian tigers are large — about 3 feet (1 m) tall at the base of the neck, reaching 10 feet (3 m) in length, and weighing from 495 to 605 pounds (225 to 275 kg) — they definitely fear humans and try to avoid them. They always remain well hidden from humans and generally stay far from human habitations.

Nevertheless, in a subcontinental area of more than 1 million sq. miles (2.6 million sq. km) that is inhabited by more than 800 million people, it is obvious that space for tigers is very scarce. The possibility for dangerous encounters between humans and tigers always exists.

The attack of a tiger is extremely sudden and rapid. It begins from a distance of 15 to 30 feet (5 to 10 m). The tiger covers this distance by running. Generally, the attacks take place at night, by solitary tigers. However, George Schaller, who has studied wild tigers in India, says that sometimes tigers belonging to the same group are active during the day and share their prey.

The attack is made after a careful calculation, which tends to minimize the chances of failure. An exceptional film shot in China has demonstrated the tiger's technique for hunting a deer. With extraordinary patience, the cat moves forward with its belly to the ground, becoming immediately motionless as soon as the deer lifts its head. Since deer have a keen sense of smell and can sense the strong odor of a predator, the tiger always approaches against the wind. When it has reached the attacking distance, it waits till the deer relaxes and peacefully starts to graze again. It is at this point that the

Opposite page: The hunting technique of the tiger is studied. *From top to bottom:* Once the tiger has smelled the prey (in this case, a wild boar), it follows and moves closer, hiding in the vegetation. When it reaches a close distance, it keeps its belly to the ground while tensing its muscles. It waits until the prey becomes completely relaxed. When it is sure to have the advantage of surprise, the tiger suddenly leaps on top of the prey and quickly kills it with a powerful bite at the base of the neck.

The tiger, unlike the lion and the leopard (but similar to the South American jaguar), likes to jump into water, and it easily swims across rivers, lakes, and even narrow arms of the sea. This is demonstrated by its presence on the island of Sri Lanka and on numerous islands of the Indonesian area.

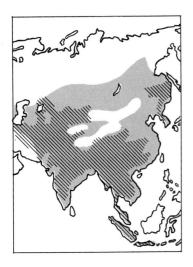

Past distribution (colored zone) and present distribution (lined zone) of the tiger is shown. The movement southward from its original area occurred in two waves —one toward the south and the other toward the southwest. The tiger circled around the uncrossable Himalayas, as can be seen in the illustration.

tiger, using the advantage of surprise, attacks with all its force, dropping the prey by striking the deer's snout with its front claws. It then sinks its teeth deeply into the prey's neck, fracturing the vertebra and tearing internal organs. The victim usually dies within a few minutes, and the tiger obtains a good supply of meat.

Generally, the tiger eats the rear parts of the prey's body, leaving the front part for the second night. If it makes a third visit to the carcass, it will eat the meat off the neck and the head, assuming that hyenas and jackals have not come to feed in the meantime.

Living with Humans

No one really knows to what extent the nocturnal habits of tigers have been influenced by the presence of humans. Certainly, the possibilities of humans and tigers living together are limited.

In India, there were from forty thousand to fifty thousand tigers at the beginning of this century. The tiger has completely disappeared from Turkey and from a large part of Siberia and China. It is rare in Iran and even in Java and Sumatra which, for a long time, were considered legendary strongholds. The decline of the tigers in India was brought about by colonial hunting parties during British rule and the need to regulate the territory dominated and controlled by such a powerful predator.

It is true that the tiger generally fears humans, and if people take a minimum amount of precaution, there will be few attacks. However, it is also true that the attacks of these rare animals can be terrifying, and even the small number of deadly attacks on individuals represents a serious problem.

In 1972, when the tiger's situation was already critical, the hunting of these animals was abolished in India, and the first national parks were established. Three wildlife protection agencies also began an active project designed to help protect the animal. These agencies were the International Union for the Conservation of Nature, the World Wildlife Fund, and the Smithsonian Institution. Their project was called "Project Tiger."

The success of this program was considerable. In 1979, seven years after the establishment of the first parks and reserves in India, official reports counted three thousand tigers in the country. Today, there are an estimated six thousand tigers in all of Asia, of which perhaps two-thirds are in India.

Unfortunately, the increase in the tiger population in India has aggravated the traditional problems associated with humans living near these animals. Today, in a total area of 2,300 sq. miles (5,957 sq. km) of protected zones, there are almost eight hundred tigers. The others live in the nonprotected forests. On the average, there is one tiger for every 2.7 to 3 sq. miles (7 to 8 sq. km) of protected land. The ideal ratio in a stable, natural balance would be one animal for every 19 to 23 sq. miles (50 to 60 sq. km).

In reality, the situation for tigers in the Indian parks resembles an overpopulated prison, and these reserves are continually violated by people who gather fruit, graze their domestic animals, and harvest the grasses. The violations are committed by poor people.

Other harmful activities have been carried out by well-meaning people who try to help conserve animals in their own misguided ways. An example of this is the case of Billy Arjun Shingh, an official of the Dudhawa

A resting tiger blends perfectly with the tall grasses of a clearing. Its dark stripes on the light background of its coat, along with the white spots on the snout, chest, and belly, together make this animal almost invisible among the dark and light patterns of the forest vegetation.

Park. For many years, Arjun tried to gradually introduce to the wild tiger cubs that had been born in captivity. He fed them buffalo meat until the age of two or three and then set them free. For a period of time, he continued to supply them daily with a certain amount of food. He gradually reduced the amount in the hope that the tigers would begin hunting on their own.

In the end, unfortunately, this procedure proved to be useless and extremely dangerous. Releasing semidomestic tigers into areas that already have a wild population does not work. One tiger cub Arjun tried to introduce began to hunt primarily humans, with which the animal had become all too familiar. Before this animal was destroyed, it killed at least twenty-two people. Another tiger, named Long Tooth, killed four people after having been introduced to the wild.

Between 1973 and 1982, in the Dudhawa and Corbett parks, the "man-eaters" seemed to have multiplied to terrifying levels. Tigers killed more than one hundred people, including many children, and several other people and livestock were wounded.

In 1984, Ramesh Bedi wrote: "In February of 1979, I stayed in a small village of straw and mud huts with the Tharu tribe near the Sharada River. The people of the village were torn by terror and resignation. In less than one year, the ferocious Mohammadi [a man-eating tiger] had killed and torn to pieces fifteen people. The Tharu tribe is nomadic, and the members live in very small groups. Therefore, every person in that village had lost at least one relative or friend. Their stories were filled with horror, pain, and anger. An exasperated young woman who had lost her husband told me that 'our skin is worth much less than the tiger's skin, and even less than its tail alone.' She was not far from the truth, since the Indian government gave five thousand rupees [about $400] to the woman whose husband was the sixth victim of Mohammadi, and she did not know how she was going to feed her 12 children."

Future Prospects

What should be done, then? First of all, like all endangered species, the tiger requires attention and protection. Project Tiger was a courageous and opportune program at a time when the tiger's situation seemed hopeless. Perhaps, the program was applied too thoroughly.

The tiger rarely eats humans, but the incidents that occur in zones populated by tigers show that it is impossible for humans to coexist peacefully with these cats. People and tigers cannot live in the same territory. They must inhabit areas separated by well-defined borders. In areas where humans and tigers are relatively close to each other, the population density of the tigers must be kept low, so they are not tempted to go beyond their borders and harm people. Humans would then not be forced to interfere in tiger territory.

Obviously, this goal is not easy to achieve in India. It would require wide-ranging and long-term social and economic programs. However, if the objective is to save the wild tiger, then a long-term project must be developed.

FOREST REPTILES AND RIVER FISHERS

The jungle is not the exclusive dominion of the large mammals or the predators. If one spends the day hiking along a river or a series of hills covered by forest, one would probably rarely encounter the large mammals or their tracks. Perhaps one would see a pair of jackals at dawn or get a quick view of a pair of fleeing deer. Maybe one would see a few tracks of a panther in the sand or hear the grunts of a lipped bear near a group of termite nests. The most frequent encounters will be with small animals. Rustling sounds will be made by small lizards fleeing to their holes and by squirrels that disappear behind the leaves of trees. One will hear the call of a variety of birds and the buzzing of different insects. One will also see the flashing colors of butterfly wings.

It would be impossible to list the numerous small inhabitants of the Indian forests. It is better to concentrate on the most characteristic inhabitants found in the jungle and present a representative picture of life there.

Cobras and Mongooses

Many kinds of lizards, especially geckos and skinks, are found in India. There are also about 230 species of snakes. Of these, about 50 are poisonous or otherwise dangerous to humans. The most well known of the poisonous snakes are the king cobra and the common cobra.

Cobras, along with the African mamba, the American coral snakes, and the Australasian sea snakes, make up a group of poisonous snakes called "proteroglyphs." These snakes have hollow fangs situated at the front of the top jaw. The fangs cannot be drawn back like the fangs of the vipers or rattlesnakes.

Their poison is strong. Every year in India, thousands of humans are killed by cobra bites. When startled, both the common cobra and the king cobra raise the front part of their bodies off the ground. They will then flatten and widen their necks, giving the impression that they have a hood and are ready to strike.

The maximum length of the common cobra is about 6 feet (2 m). The length of the king cobra can at times exceed 13 feet (4 m). The largest king cobras weigh from 11 to 13 pounds (5 to 6 kg).

The common cobra feeds primarily on rodents, sometimes on small birds. The king cobra is specialized

Opposite page: A glassed cobra is photographed with its charmer. The cobra is widespread in the Indo-Malaysian region. It is found in humid areas with rich vegetation, as well as in arid areas. It often gets close to areas of human habitation while searching for rodents, which are its most common prey.

Seen here are the stages in the fight between a cobra and a mongoose. The mongoose gets the better of the cobra due to its quickness and the perfect coordination of its movements. At first the mongoose dodges the snake's attacks, tiring the reptile in the process (*top*); then, suddenly, the mongoose counterattacks at the precise moment when the cobra has just completed a missed strike; the mongoose seizes the cobra with its jaws, killing it (*bottom*). It is hard for the cobra to bite the mongoose. Even if the cobra succeeds in biting the mongoose, it is improbable that it would kill it.

as a hunter of other snakes and is the only species of its group that builds a nest. The female piles dead leaves and other plant material to cover its eggs, and then it coils itself on top of this nest to protect them. Anyone coming near a female guarding its eggs almost certainly will have a terrible experience. The large cobra is easily provoked. It can raise its head more than 3 feet (1 m) off the ground in a menacing pose, and it strikes with great accuracy.

The gray Indian mongoose and the minor mongoose are among the few animals capable of facing and killing a cobra. When these animals encounter one, especially a common cobra, their fur stands straight out, and they move slowly toward the snake. When the cobra strikes,

the mongoose ably dodges to the side and starts over. After a number of attacks, the cobra begins to tire, and its movements become slower. At this point, the mongoose begins to counterattack. It tries to seize the cobra by the head or the neck at the precise instant just after the cobra's strike. Attacks and counterattacks might be repeated several times. Eventually, the mongoose succeeds in killing the cobra.

The mongoose's best defense against the cobra is its extraordinary quickness. Another advantage is its thick fur, which the cobra may strike without puncturing the mongoose's skin. Even if the cobra succeeds in biting the mongoose, it usually does not succeed in killing it. The mongoose is resistant to the cobra's poison, and its

Indian rock python coils on the bare ground. Generally, the Indian python does not exceed 19 feet (6 m) in length. During the day, it finds refuge in abandoned animal dens and among the roots of trees. However, it can also be found in open areas that are shaded. At night, it moves in search of birds and small mammals, which are its usual prey, or it may remain waiting for prey near a pool of water. The python has been widely hunted due to the beauty of its prized skin. In several areas its numbers have been considerably reduced. Many times, it is killed solely in reaction to the fear it causes.

resistance increases with each nonfatal cobra bite the mongoose receives.

The Python

While the cobras are feared because of their poison, there are also nonpoisonous, constricting snakes that cause terror in India, or at least anxiety, even when seen in a zoo. A typical example of these constricting "monsters" is the gigantic rock python.

Despite its name, the Indian rock python inhabits primarily forest or brushy zones. It often stays near ponds and marshes, where it submerges itself when disturbed. This gigantic snake can reach a length of 20 feet (6 m) and a weight of about 220 pounds (100 kg). It

The well-known ability of snakes to swallow the prey whole (which is often much larger than the snakes's diameter) is due to a series of body adaptations. The square bone, which connects the jawbone to the skull, is mobile. It allows the jaw to move forward or backward. The jawbone is not hardened in the center. Its two parts are united by an elastic ligament that permits them to open apart from each other. There are other adaptations. The ear, for example, lacks a drum and an Eustachian tube (which would not be able to withstand such swallowings). If the snake had eyelids, they would also be damaged by these swallowings, so instead of eyelids, the snake's eyes are covered with a transparent scale. This enables the snake to see around it constantly.

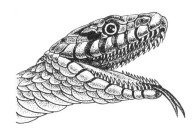

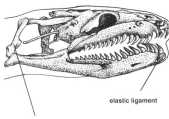

elastic ligament

square bone

square bone

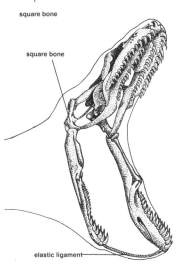

elastic ligament

feeds mostly on mammals, from the size of mice up to small wild boar and deer fawns.

Once the prey is bitten, the python coils around the victim and rapidly suffocates it by blocking its breathing and blood circulation. It does not crush its prey, as some people have mistakenly reported.

Despite what has been said about the danger of these snakes in regard to humans, the python definitely tries in every way to avoid people. A large python coiled up in bushes in the Bharatpur reserve decided to threaten a photographer only when he had approached to within 3 feet (1 m). After opening its mouth and raising its neck, the gigantic reptile rapidly retreated and disappeared into the forest. Its gigantic coils were an incredible sight.

Although they are able to adapt to a variety of habitats, pythons need vast and undisturbed zones. They must be able to hunt without being noticed by humans, who kill them for their meat and skin and for the fear they cause. Today, these conditions are becoming rare in India. Despite legal restrictions protecting them, pythons have been wiped out in all the areas that have been deforested and overpopulated by humans.

Snake Charmers

The snake charmer is probably one of the images that comes to mind when a person thinks about India. Charmers perform in the streets of large cities, using cobras and pythons. The pythons are usually held around the neck, while the cobras appear from inside baskets. While the charmer plays a flute, as many as ten, or even twenty, snakes may rise up out of their baskets.

Charmers generally use some tricks. Even when they do not remove the channeled fangs of the cobra, they periodically empty the poison glands and often submerge the snakes in cold water to calm them. Actually, the charmers have a considerable knowledge of the physiology and behavior of these snakes. They condition them through a patient study of their responses and not with music — snakes are almost deaf because their ears are covered by scales.

Lizards

The most common lizards in India are the small calot lizards. They are crested and resemble small

A wary calot lizard perches on top of a stone wall. Calot lizards, like chameleons and the other members of the same family, change their color. This is not done so much for camouflage as to signal the presence of one lizard to other members of the same species. It also serves to show the state of their excitement.

dragons. They can be found among the brush of the forest, in public gardens, and on the walls surrounding the buildings of the embassy district of Delhi.

On the average, they are smaller and more agile than European lizards and feed almost exclusively on small insects. To remain active, they need high temperatures and humidity. The calot lizards belong to the family Agamidae. This group includes lizards with a wide variety of shapes. They are commonly found throughout Asia, Africa, and Australia. One species is also found in Europe.

The monitor lizard is the largest lizard on earth. The most common species in India is the Bengala monitor. It lives in environments that are rich in vegetation, and it often makes its home in hollow trees.

The monitor is closely related to the reptiles that are the ancestors of the snakes, and their habits and structure are very much like those of the snakes. For example, the monitor usually swallows its prey whole and has a forked and mobile tongue. The Bengala monitor feeds on animals up to the size of chickens, and it readily steals eggs from bird nests.

The animal in the photo, a gavial, has a rarely seen bright green color. Because it has lived in a small pool of water, there are many microscopic encrustations of algae covering large sections of its body.

Gavials, Crocodiles, and River Dolphins

Any book dealing with Indian reptiles would not be complete without at least a mention of the Ganges gavial. This is a unique crocodile that reaches 16 to 20 feet (5 to 6 m) in length and is completely harmless to humans. It has a long, narrow snout that is well adapted for the capture of fish and crustaceans. The slender snout of the gavial moves more easily in the water than the snout of the marsh crocodile, which is also found throughout India.

The long, thin jaws of the gavial have many teeth that curve slightly inward. Each tooth is used as a harpoon to pierce fish. The gavial feeds almost exclusively on fish, although it occasionally captures aquatic birds or small mammals that approach the water to drink. Sometimes rings and other ornaments of humans have been found in the stomachs of gavials, but these were certainly from dead bodies that were thrown into rivers instead of being buried or cremated (a widespread practice of several Indian religious groups).

THE SLOPES OF THE HIMALAYAS

The largest chain of mountains in the world extends across the entire Asian continent, from the Mediterranean to the Bering Sea. The central part of this chain, north of India, contains many peaks reaching elevations of between 6,500 and 29,500 feet (2,000 to 9,000 m).

Like the Alps, the Himalayas originated from the joining of continents during the Tertiary period. The Himalayan chain separates tropical Asia from the colder and more temperate parts of the continent. It reduces to a minimum the exchanges between plants and animals on each side of these mountains. Even the migratory birds of western and central Siberia generally prefer the longer flight to winter in Africa rather than crossing the Himalayas.

The Himalayas are large and complex. It is impossible to adequately describe in a short book the large variety of unique plants and animals they contain. For this reason, what follows is only a brief description of the southern parts of these mountains, an area subject to the influences of the vegetation and animals of the Indian subcontinent.

Vegetation of the Lower Slopes

When one begins to climb from the Ganges River plain toward the Himalayan villages of Uttar Pradesh or Kashmir, the first sensation is that of entering an almost inaccessible world. It has been much less changed by humans than the areas below.

At a certain elevation, the deciduous (leaf-dropping) monsoon forest begins. This can be seen from a bus as it climbs the steep mountain roads. The forest has the appearance of the broad-leaved forests of southern Europe, but it has very different species of trees.

As one moves higher in elevation along the Ganges River valley, he or she will see spectacular gorges and clear streams running between enormous masses of rocks. This is still the habitat of the langur monkey, the leopards, and other typical Indian animals that also live in the rare forest areas of the plains.

Areas of forested mountains alternate with bare mountains, marked by traces of terracings that are in complete ruin. Here, humans deforested the mountains in an attempt to cultivate the difficult land. Gradually, however, these areas were abandoned and the popula-

Opposite page: Three yaks, part of an expedition caravan, climb the snowy peaks of the Himalayas. The yak is an important domestic animal for the people inhabiting the Tibetan plateau. It survives elevations of over 19,000 feet (6,000 m), and its meat, lard, and milk are the basis of the diet of the people here. Its hide and wool provide warmth in a harsh climate. Its skin is used for tents and boats. Even its dung is used, both as fertilizer and fuel.

A rhododendron tree stands out against the Annapurna peak. In the Himalayas, the rhododendron tree occupies a band of elevation similar to that which it occupies in the Alps. First it is mixed with conifer trees (cone-bearing evergreens), and then a little higher up, it grows in almost pure stands. In the Alps, rhododendrons are shrubs that are no taller than 3.5 feet (1 m). Those in the Himalayas are true trees that reach a height of over 32 feet (10 m). There are at least seven hundred species of rhododendrons in Asia.

tion moved to large cities, leaving behind rocky slopes covered by a few shrubs and spurge plants.

Around the sacred city of Devprag, where a branch of the Alaknanda River merges with the Bhagirati River to form the Ganges, the mountains are dry and bare. The vegetation becomes even more sparse up to 6,500 feet (2,000 m) of elevation, where the forests begin once more.

From Deciduous Broadleaves to Rhododendrons

Pauri is a typical village in the Uttar Pradesh region, located at an elevation of 6,500 feet (2,000 m) and within sight of the Himalayas. Around this village, one can notice the principal characteristics of the forests that cover these slopes. Along a 15-mile (24-km) route from the village, one crosses a magnificent forest of oaks and rhododendrons that reach 33 feet (10 m) in height. The underbrush is thick with ferns, mosses, lichens, and orchids, which give it an exotic appearance.

This forest is populated by birds similar to those of Europe: the crested titmouse with yellow cheeks, the red-headed codibugnolo, and chestnut-colored and reddish yellow woodpeckers. Although these birds have

crested titmouse, yellow cheeks

codibugnolo titmouse, red head

blue magpie, red beaked

tragopan pheasant

the same genus as their European relatives, they belong to different species.

In addition to these birds, there are also species that are primarily tropical. These include the incredible firebird, the male of which has showy red-and-black plumage. When it flies among the forest trees, it is one of the most extraordinary sights that can be seen in all of tropical Asia.

A short distance above Pauri, the forest is dominated by conifer (cone-bearing) trees. These include Indian pines, cypresses, cedars, and larches, as well as some oaks. The oaks become rare a little higher in elevation, where the forest is primarily composed of the needle-leaved trees, or conifers.

A little higher, the conifer forest is mixed with rhododendrons, until finally it is composed only of rhododendrons. In the area between Assam, Burma, and Tibet, one can find seven hundred species of rhododendron trees and shrubs. The rhododendrons, with their spectacular and abundant flowers, are one of the most extraordinary attractions of this region. In the spring, the forests suddenly become clothed in the various colors (white, pink, red, violet, and yellow) of the different species of this tree.

This flowering is one of the most extraordinary spectacles on earth. According to several travelers who have seen the sight, it alone can easily justify a trip to this region.

The Animals

Several interesting animals are characteristic of this region. Besides the many macaco monkeys that seem to be particularly large in this area, mention should be made of the brawny Tibetan black bear. This bear is characterized by a white half-moon on its chest. There are also several kinds of otters, yellow throated martens, and Himalayan weasels.

The movements of the wild goats and sheep at these high elevations are followed by an exceptional predator, the snow leopard, or irbis. In the summer, it climbs to 16,400 feet (5,000 m) in elevation. In the winter, it comes down to 6,500 feet (2,000 m). It is light gray on its upper parts and almost white on its lower parts. Its spots are less noticeable than those of the leopards of the plains and the hills, and its fur is quite thick. Besides wild goats

Flying squirrels play among the branches. The structure of the skin flaps, which connect the front legs to the rear legs and which allow the squirrel to glide, is identical in all the numerous species of this group of animals. This skin flap (membrane) is attached to the wrist by means of cartilage. When the squirrel is not gliding, the flap is folded back against the forearm by a particular muscle. "In flight," the cartilage and flaps are extended to the maximum by a thumb muscle.

and sheep, it feeds on bobak marmots (rodents), magpies, and mountain pheasants, and, occasionally, it also preys on livestock.

Little is known about the life of this animal. The number of scientists who have seen the snow leopard in the wild can be counted on two hands. Generally, the harshness of the territory it inhabits, its nocturnal habits, and its extreme caution in hiding have contributed to the myths that surround this beautiful animal. These are similar to myths of the abominable snowman, or bigfoot.

Recently, a young British scientist researched this animal over a period of three years. He was able to gather only traces and indirect proof of its presence and activities, without ever encountering the animal.

However, several Asian zoologists were more fortunate. One of them, the Chinese scientist Show-Chen Ruang, discovered that this animal lives in pairs or family groups, and it maintains a territory about the size of an entire mountain valley. Two to four offspring are born in the spring after a gestation of about three months. The young remain near the mother throughout the following winter.

A cave or rocky gorge is often permanently used as a den, with the result that it becomes covered by a layer of shed fur from successive moltings (fur sheddings). This fur is tamped down and compressed, reaching a

The minor panda inhabits bamboo and rhododendron forests. It is smaller and less specialized than the large panda, but it is more common and widespread. It is so much like the raccoon that many zoologists consider it a member of the raccoon family. However, it is much less adapted to the presence of humans and the resulting habitat changes than the American raccoon. It is basically vegetarian in its eating habits.

thickness of one-half inch (13 mm).

The hunting system of the snow leopard consists of a cautious approach followed by a short and sudden attack. According to Show-Chen Ruang, this animal is capable of leaps of 33 feet (10 m) and can jump over obstacles that are 10 to 13 feet (3 to 4 m) high.

Since the fur of this leopard is highly prized, the animal has been widely hunted for years. Today, it is protected in all of the areas of its distribution, although this is hard to enforce in many localities.

The minor panda inhabits the areas of Sikkim and Nepal above 4,500 feet (1,372 m). This animal resembles

Illustration of the eating habits of the lammergeier. *From left to right:* The lammergeier feeds primarily on the skin and bones of carcasses that have been fleshed by vultures. Its extraordinary ability permits it to commit acts of "piracy." It steals small prey from flying birds of prey after having disoriented them by striking them with its wings. The lammergeier prefers to eat bone marrow and sometimes drops whole bones from the air to break them on rocks below to expose the marrow.

a raccoon. It feeds primarily on succulent (juicy) plants, roots, leaves, and fruit, and it also eats a small amount of insects and bird eggs.

Flying squirrels present another group of unique mammals. There are at least two Himalayan species that are found up to the limit of the tree cover. The red flying squirrel is about 18 inches (46 cm) long, excluding the tail. The Kahmir flying squirrel is a little smaller, measuring only 10 to 12 inches (25 to 30 cm) in length, excluding the tail.

The flying squirrels are lightweight animals with flattened, bushy tails. They have two unique extensions of skin along their sides that connect the front legs to the rear legs. These extensions act as a sort of parachute. This skin is covered with fur, making it more attractive than the bare skin flaps of bat wings. With these unique flaps, the flying squirrel can glide long distances from one tree to another.

As for birds, the Himalayan area has many interesting species. These include the beautiful blue magpie with a red beak, the blue whistling thrush, and some spectacular pheasants. Some of these are the tragopan pheasant, the male of which is reddish colored with small white spots, and the incredible lofofor pheasant. The lofofor has an iridescent (rainbowlike) plumage that changes into at least nine different colors, which the male proudly shows during its mating walk.

The large lammergeier is as spectacular as the birds just described. It is very different from other vultures, as it has several colors and is bearded. It also has habits unlike those of any other bird of prey. For example, this bird feeds on bone marrow, the soft material that fills bone cavities. The lammergeier obtains this food by dropping the long bones of the carcasses of large animals on rocks to break them.

GUIDE TO AREAS OF NATURAL INTEREST

Nature lovers are highly attracted to the national parks and nature reserves of the Indian subcontinent. The parks and reserves can be visited by car or boat or on foot. They are well organized in regard to guide services and lodging possibilities. The lodgings are always adequate, even though they do not compare with the high standards (and costs) of lodgings in the parks of East Africa.

As a rule, the tourist who is seriously interested in visiting natural environments should spend at least three days in the most important parks and one day in the minor parks. Some areas, such as bird sanctuaries, should be visited for longer periods, possibly for an entire vacation. This is especially the case when one has a serious interest in nature photography.

A good pair of binoculars is a necessary traveling companion, particularly for those interested in bird watching. Another important piece of equipment is a 35mm reflex camera with a 300 to 500mm telephoto lens. For persons interested only in landscapes and lighter equipment, a small 35mm range finder camera is advisable.

In the forest one should wear light clothing, avoiding the exposure of large areas of skin to mosquitoes and horseflies. One should also have a good supply of insect repellant and vaccinations against cholera, typhus, and malaria. It would also be helpful to take some simple sanitary precautions against amoebic dysentery and other intestinal infections caused by bacteria. These infections result from drinking infected water or eating certain raw foods. It is preferable to drink only boiled water and eat only cooked food. Raw vegetables and peeled fruit should be avoided.

The means of local transportation are very low in cost, but they certainly are not up to the standards some tourists are used to in their own countries. For these people, the most convenient solution may be airline flights and taxis, although this is less adventurous and more costly.

A useful source of information for planning a nature trip to the Indian subcontinent is the Bombay Natural Historical Society. It is an old scientific and conservationist society. Since 1886, it has published a magazine recognized as the most authoritative source of information on the plants and animals of the subcontinent.

Opposite page: A clump of giant bamboo grows in a natural reserve in India. National parks and reserves are numerous and well organized in India. By visiting them, one can get a good idea of the animals and vegetation of various regions.

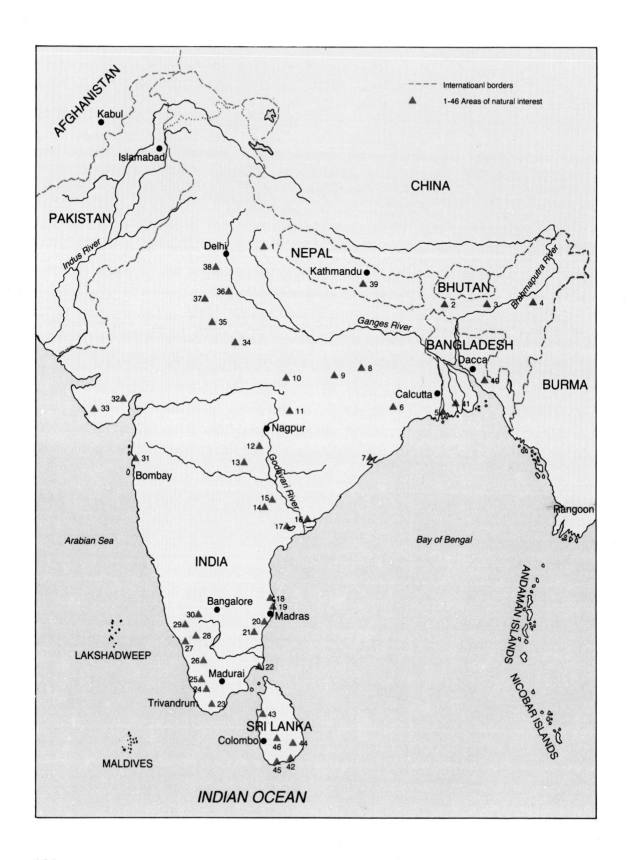

INDIA

Corbett (1)

Jaldapara (2)

Manas (3)

Corbett was the first national park established in India and the first area assigned to "Project Tiger" (1973). It extends across 200 sq. miles (518 sq. km) of hills covered by deciduous forests at the foot of the Himalayas in the region of Uttar Pradesh.

This park is crossed by the Ramganga River and its numerous tributaries, and it has a large number and variety of animals. These include tigers, leopards, elephants, jackals, sambar, chital, marsh and hog deer, muntjac, wild boar, rabbits, and porcupines. There are at least six hundred species of birds, including hornbills, parrots, storks, herons, spoonbills, cranes, and ibises. Some of the reptiles are the marsh crocodile, the gavial, and the python.

From Delhi, the park can be reached by taking a train 150 miles (241 km) to Ramngar and continuing by bus 30 miles (50 km) to Dhikala. In Dhikala, there are several rest houses. The park is open from November to May. The park is closed from June to October.

The Jaldapara sanctuary is located at the foot of the Bhutan hills and is crossed by the Torsa River. The area is primarily covered by tall grasses. It is one of the last refuges of the Indian rhinoceros. Among the other animals at Jaldapara are tigers, leopards, elephants, various species of deer, and numerous birds, including the Bengala bustard and the minor marabu. The best time to visit is from December to May. The closest airport is Bagdogra, and the closest train station is in Madari Hat.

Like Jaldapara, the Manas Tiger Reserve extends along the foot of the Bhutan hills over an area of 1,000 sq. miles (2,600 sq. km). It is crossed by various streams, including the Manas River and its tributaries, the Beki and the Hakna rivers. The area is characterized by riverbeds with multicolored rocks.

The main vegetation is deciduous forest. More or less all the large animals of the region are found in this park — tigers, leopards, wild buffalo, and Indian rhinoceroses. There are also several interesting animals that are not found elsewhere. These are the Assam rabbit (whose habits are still relatively unknown), the pygmy wild boar (which is only 10 inches (25 cm) tall at the base of the neck), and the tree shrew.

The many birds of the park include two types of calao birds. At dawn, from the lodges of Mothanguri, one can see these birds flying toward the forest. At dusk, they can be seen flying in twos and threes, returning to the river.

Mothanguri can be reached by car on the Barpeta Road. It is 25 miles (40 km) from the railroad station and 105 miles (169 km) from the Gauhati airport.

Kaziranga (4)

The Kaziranga National Park occupies an area of about 165 sq. miles (427 sq. km) along the Brahmaputra River. The park includes marshes full of water hyacinths, savannas with tall grasses, and an evergreen forest. The most notable animals are the Indian rhinoceros and the wild buffalo. There are also marsh deer, hog deer, tigers, leopards, lipped bears, elephants, and otters. There are also many aquatic birds, such as pelicans, herons, and cormorants.

The reserve is open from January to May, when the Brahmaputra River has a low water level. During this period one may stay in lodges, which can be reached by car from the airports of Jorhat (57 miles or 92 km away) or Gauhati (130 miles or 209 km away). Either four-wheel drive vehicles or elephants can be rented. The large animals at Kaziranga can easily be seen even during short excursions.

Sunderbans (5)

The Sunderbans Tiger Reserve is located in an immense swamp of mangrove trees where the Ganges River meets the ocean. It covers an area of 965 sq. miles (2,500 sq. km), one-third of which lies in India and two-thirds in Bangladesh. Its name comes from the local word *sundri*, which means mangrove tree. Here chital deer, wild boar, and tigers are abundant. The tigers are particularly feared for their aggressive behavior toward people. Lodgings for tourists are not available. The Sunderbans in the territory of Bangladesh is also protected.

Simlipal (6)

The vast area of 1,000 sq. miles (2,600 sq. km) of the Simlipal Tiger Reserve is located in the hills of Mayurbhanj. It is rich with deciduous forests, clearings, rivers, and waterfalls. Among the mammals found in this reserve are tigers, leopards, elephants, gaurs, and chital deer. One of the more common birds of these forests is the religious grackle, which can imitate the human voice. The closest railroad station is at Baripada, which is 30 miles (48 km) away. The nearest airport is at Bhubaneshwar, which is 217 miles (350 km) away. The park has a rest house.

Chilka (7)

The Chilka sanctuary is a coastal lagoon with a large number of aquatic birds, both resident and migratory. These include flamingos, ducks, geese, and shorebirds. One can often see dolphins in the sea that borders the sanctuary. The best time to visit the Chilka sanctuary is during the winter season, when most of the migratory birds arrive.

There are rest houses at Barkul and Rambha. The nearest railroad station is at Balugaon.

Hazaribagh (8)

The Hazaribagh sanctuary is located near the national highway that runs from Ranchi to Calcutta. Most of its inhabitants are birds. Worthy of mention is the goatsucker, which appears around the rest house after dusk. There are not many large animals here, and they are usually seen only at night. Sambar deer, striped hyenas, leopards, and tigers are all found in this area. The sanctuary can be reached by car. It is 70 miles (113 km) from Ranchi and 30 miles (48 km) from Kodama.

Palamau (9)

The Palamau Tiger Reserve has an area of 360 sq. miles (932 sq. km). It is between the Koel and the Auranga rivers. It includes ample areas of deciduous forest.

During the very hot summer, the wells are surrounded by such animals as tigers, leopards, wildcats, langur and rhesus monkeys, elephants, gaurs, sambar and chital deer, and nilgau antelope. The birds include peacocks, parakeets, white-necked storks, and francolins.

An airport and railroad station are at Ranchi, 112 miles (180 km) from the reserve. From Ranchi, the rest houses of Palamau (Betla) can be reached by bus.

Bandogarh (10)

On the 40 sq. miles (104 sq. km) of the Bandogarh National Park one can find tigers, leopards, lipped bears, gaurs, sambar, chital and muntjac deer, nilgau antelope, chinkara, and wild boar.

The closest railroad station is at Umaria. From here one can take a bus. Cars and elephants can be rented.

A well in the dry region of India. It is hard to limit oneself to natural attractions on a trip to India, since this country offers many interesting aspects. In India, it is impossible to understand the natural environments without studying the life of its people.

Kanha (11)

The Kanha Tiger Reserve was an old hunting reserve, which became a national park in 1955. It has a large population of marsh deer. In the 1970s, it was used as a special reserve for Project Tiger. Its 750-sq.-mile (1,945-sq.-km) area is covered by deciduous forests (including bamboo, small palms, and the majestic sal trees) and vast fields. Tigers, leopards, jackals, wild dogs (dhole), gaur, reedbuck antelope, langur monkeys, plus sambar, chital, barasingha, and muntjac deer are common. Among the more spectacular birds are peacocks, aquatic jays, vultures, and crested snake eagles.

The best time to visit the Kanha Tiger Reserve is from February to June. The closest airport is that of Nagpur (Maharashtra), which is 162 miles (261 km) from Kanha. The most convenient railroad station is 107 miles (170 km) away at Jabalpur. From here, Kanha can be reached by bus.

Taroba (12)

The small national park of Taroba, which extends for 45 sq. miles (117 sq. km), is located in an area of mixed deciduous forests around a circular lake. Lodges have been built on the shores of this lake.

Some of the trees growing here are bamboo, teak, mango, mohwa, jamun, and gardenia. Tigers are scarce, but leopards are numerous. They can sometimes be seen at night by car. Unlike other parks, night excursions by car are permitted here. Jackals, wild dogs, civets, gaurs, nilgau antelope, muntjac, chital and sambar deer, wild boar, and crocodiles can all be seen in the Taroba Park.

The park is well furnished with lodges. It is 24 miles (39 km) from the Chandrapur railroad station and 125 miles (201 km) from the Nagpur airport. The most favorable time to visit is the summer.

Kawal (13)

The Kawal sanctuary is located in a hilly deciduous forest with an environment similar to that of the Taroba National Park. It covers an area of 320 sq. miles (830 sq. km), and it includes gaur, sambar, chital and muntjac deer, nilgau antelope, Indian gazelles, wild boar, and langur and macaco monkeys. Such carnivores as tigers, leopards, hyenas, and lipped bears are also present, but they are rarely seen during the day. The closest airport is that of Hyderabad, which is 156 miles (252 km) away. The nearest railroad station is at Mancherial. The most favorable period to visit is from November to May.

Pakhal (14)

Eturnagaram (15)

Coringa (16)

Kolleru (17)

Nelapattu (18)

Pulicat (19)

Guindy (20)

The Pakhal sanctuary is a flatland forest with a broad lake similar to the lake at Kawal. It covers an area of 324 sq. miles (839 sq. km). The airport at Hyderbad is 162 miles (261 km) away, and the railway station at Warangal is 37 miles (60 km) away.

The Eturnagaram sanctuary is a deciduous forest of 320 sq. miles (829 sq. km). It is similar to that of Kawal in physical features, kinds of wildlife, and visiting season. The nearest airport is 140 miles (225 km) away, at Hyderabad. The nearest railroad station is at Kazipet, which is 50 miles (80 km) away. The sanctuary only has one rest house and a vehicle that can be rented.

Located on the delta of the Godavari River, the Coringa sanctuary has many aquatic birds. The rare porous crocodile lives in this area, along with otters and fishing cats. Rest houses and a railroad station are available at Kakinada, 12 miles (20 km) away.

The vast lake of Kolleru is a bird sanctuary populated with ducks, storks, and herons from October to January. At one time numerous pelicans came to fish, nesting near Aredu. That colony has been abandoned. The closest city, Eluru, is 6 miles (10 km) away. It has a rest house and a railroad station.

Large colonies of pelicans, cormorants, storks, white ibises, and herons nest on the trees in the small coastal village of Nelapattu, at the center of this sanctuary. It is 75 miles (120 km) from the Madras airport, and only a half mile from the Madras Vijayawada national highway. In the nearby village of Sulurpetta, there is a rest house.

In autumn through winter (October to March), the vast coastal lagoon of Pulicat is populated with flamingos, curlews, avocets, gulls, and ducks. The birds that reside here year-round are the pelicans, wood storks, spoonbills, and herons. The nearest airport is that of Madras (60 miles, 97 km away), and the railroad station is at Tada.

Guindy is the smallest national park in India with an area of just 1 sq. mile (2.6 sq. km). It is practically inside the city of Madras. It includes a zoo and a snake house. It has reedbuck antelope, chital deer, mongooses, anteaters and many birds. It can easily be reached by city buses from Madras.

Vedanthangal (21)

Vedanthangal is one of the oldest sanctuaries established for the protection of aquatic birds. In a small, wooded area there are nests of cormorants, snakebirds, herons, storks, ibises, and spoonbills. The best time to visit is from November to December. There is a rest house near the sanctuary. The nearest airport is 50 miles (80 km) away, at Meenambakkam (Madras).

Point Calimere (22)

The Point Calimere sanctuary is a small protected zone. It covers an area of only 6.5 sq. miles (17 sq. km), and it faces the island of Sri Lanka. The sandy beach is covered by a peculiar vegetation, while further inland is a bushy jungle typical of the arid zones. There is also a large saltwater lagoon. Several small islands face the coast.

The most notable animals are the flocks of flamingos that come here to nest. There are also many other aquatic birds, such as gulls and pelicans. Dolphins often come close to the shore. Inland one can find reedbuck antelope, chital deer, and macacos.

The railroad station of Vedaranyam is very close, while the Tiruchi airport is 144 miles (232 km) away. One can rent boats at the sanctuary. The best months for visiting are December and January. It is possible to obtain lodging at the rest house by writing in advance.

Mundanthurai (23)

The Mundanthurai sanctuary is a real paradise for botanists. The 222 sq. miles (575 sq. km) of virgin forest receive over 78 inches (2,000 mm) of rain per year. Here one can find many interesting species of full-grown trees. There are tigers, leopards, lipped bears, chital and sambar deer (all nocturnal and rarely seen), as well as four species of macaco and langur monkeys.

Mundanthurai can be reached by bus from the railroad station of Tirunelveli, which is 28 miles (45 km) away. The Madurai airport is 126 miles (203 km) away. The best period to visit is from September to November.

Periyar (24)

The Periyar Tiger Reserve was the eleventh reserve of Project Tiger. Its 300 sq. miles (777 sq. km) extend around an artificial lake that is surrounded by beautiful forests. Despite the label "Tiger Reserve," this is an ideal protected zone for the Indian elephant. In no other Asian park or reserve is it possible to observe these animals in such a large number and in so many varied circumstances. There are also gaurs, sambar and muntjac deer, tigers, leopards, langur and macaco monkeys, and many aquatic and forest birds.

The best time to visit the reserve is from February to May. There are several lodgings available at Periyar, and rental boats are available. The closest airport is that of Madurai. It is 87 miles (140 km) away. From there one can take a bus to Kumili, which is very close to the reserve. The closest railroad station is Kottayam, and that is 70 miles (112 km) from Kumili.

Eravikulam (25)

The Eravikulam Rajamalai Park extends over Mount Anaimudi (8,800 feet/2,695 m), the highest peak in southern India. The Nilgiri wild goat, which is now protected, is found here. There are also macaco and langur monkeys, giant squirrels, tigers, leopards, elephants, gaurs, and the sambar and muntjac deer.

The best time to visit is from October to April. The nearest airport is 89 miles (143 km) away at Cochin. The Alwaye railroad station is 76 miles (123 km) away in Alwaye. The park is 7 miles (12 km) from Munnar. Several rest houses are available at Rajamalai.

Anaimalai (26)

Most of the forests in the Anaimalai sanctuary are evergreen. There are many animals, including langur and macaco monkeys, as well as many interesting birds. Lodgings are available near the sanctuary, and elephants and cars can be rented. The closest airport is 50 miles (80 km) away at Coimbatore, and there is a railroad station at Pollachi, 22 miles (35 km) away.

Mudumalai (27)

The 115 sq. miles (300 sq. km) of the Mudumalai sanctuary cover different types of forests. These include humid and dry deciduous forests and evergreen forests with teak and bejal trees. The animals are similar to those of the nearby Bandipur park. Elephants and gaurs, plus chital, sambar and muntjac deer, and macaco and langur monkeys, giant squirrels, flying squirrels, wild dogs, tigers, and leopards can be found in the forests.

Among the notable birds are the drongo of paradise, trogons, religious grackles, and hornbills. Monitor

A nectar bird feeds on the flower of a
Bouganvillea (a plant originally from
South Africa). These beautiful and tiny
birds are widespread in India and are
commonly seen in the countryside.

lizards are common, especially near termite nests along the road that goes from Masinagudi to the electrical plant of Moyar. Cobras and pythons are also common.

The best periods for visiting are from March to June and from September to October. The closest airport is at Coimbatore, and it is 100 miles (160 km) away. There are lodgings at Masinagudi, Theppakkadu, and Abhayaranyan. It is possible to rent cars or elephants.

Bandipur (28)

The Bandipur Tiger Reserve is located in the southernmost part of the Karnataka region. The Moyar River separates it from the Mudumalai sanctuary. It extends over an area of 270 sq. miles (700 sq. km) in a hilly zone covered by forests. Bandipur is the most famous reserve in India. This is due more to the elephants than the tigers. Here elephants can be easily observed from close range. There are also many sambar, chital, muntjac, and rat deer. Several gaurs have survived the disastrous epidemic of 1968. Tigers and leopards are active only at night, and they are very difficult to spot. Wild dogs (dhole) are frequently encountered.

Other common animals are lipped bears, porcupines, giant squirrels, and langur and macaco monkeys. Some of the notable birds are peacocks, jungle cocks, green fruit-eating pigeons, parakeets, parrots, and cuckoo pheasants. Some of the reptiles are the aquatic turtles, pythons and monitor lizards.

Bandipur is one of the best-equipped reserves for tourists. The lodges are comfortable, and it is possible to rent both cars and elephants to tour the forest. The closest airport is 118 miles (190 km) away at Bangalore. There is bus service to the railroad station at Mysore, 50 miles (80 km) away.

Ranganathitoo (29)

The Ranganathitoo sanctuary is a relatively small protected zone, but it is noted for its magnificent scenery.

At the elevation of the city of Srirangapatna, the Kaveri River divides into numerous branches and forms a series of small islands. Here, among the reeds, tall grasses, and trees, such birds as cormorants, snakebirds, herons, storks, white ibises, and spoonbills nest. There is also a large colony of fruit bats, and the river is full of crocodiles.

Nagarhole (30)

Borivili (31)

Velavadar (32)

Gir (33)

The nearest airport, which is 68 miles (110 km) away, is at Bangalore. A railroad station and lodgings can be found at Mysore. From there Srirangapatna can be easily reached by bus.

The Nagarhole sanctuary is a vast deciduous forest with many species of trees, including the ebony tree. The underbrush is dense, except for certain areas devoted to the cultivation of teak trees. The area is 220 sq. miles (570 sq. km). The area has many herds of gaur, elephants, wild dogs, and sambar, chital, muntjac, and rat deer.

Tigers and leopards remain hidden in the dense jungle and are rarely seen. The best time to visit is from October to March. The nearest airport is at Bagalore, which is 137 miles (220 km) away, and there is a railroad station at Mysore.

The Borivili National Park is a small park of only 26 sq. miles (68 sq. km) located near Bombay. A deciduous forest inhabited by sambar deer, wild boar, langur monkeys, and many types of birds surrounds the lake of this park. The nearest airport is at Santa Cruz, and the closest railroad station is at Borivili.

The Velavadar National Park is a relatively small protected zone. It was set aside primarily for the conservation of reedbuck antelope. Wolves and other animals also inhabit the park. Lodgings as well as a railroad station and an airport are found at Bhavnagar, 40 miles (65 km) from the park. One-day trips can be organized from this town.

The Gir National Park is the only refuge for the Asian lion. Only 10 percent of its 545 sq. miles (1,412 sq. km) is covered by deciduous forests. The predominant tree is the teak. The abundant clearings are covered with tall grasses and a few trees.

All 200 of the world's population of Asian lions are in the park. There are about 200 leopards, numerous striped hyenas, about 8,000 chital deer, and a smaller number of sambar deer. There are 2,000 nilgau antelope and 1,000 four-horned antelope. Wild boar, Indian gazelles, and langur monkeys also live in this park.

Shivpuri (34)

Ranthambhar (35)

Bharatpur (36)

The Shivpuri National Park is located in a deciduous forest. It is inhabited by nilgau antelope, Indian gazelles, four-horned antelope, sambal and chital deer, wild boar, reedbuck antelope, and perhaps several tigers. Many demoiselle cranes can be found on the shores of the lake. The best period to visit is from January to June, although after March the weather is very hot. There is an airport and a railroad station at Gwalior. This town has a regular bus service to Shivpuri, which is about 75 miles (120 km) away, where there are lodgings.

The Ranthambhar Tiger Reserve is relatively small, but it is particularly interesting and well preserved. Its 135 sq. miles (350 sq. km) are situated on rolling hills with steep slopes. The slopes and the valleys are covered by a deciduous vegetation that is typical of arid zones. The crests of the hills are characterized by a sparse deciduous vegetation typical of semiarid zones.

The area has chital and sambar deer, nilgau antelope, Indian gazelles, wild boar, and langur monkeys. Among the carnivores are tigers, leopards, jackals, striped hyenas, lipped bears, mongooses, and civets. There are also many different kinds of birds.

The best period to visit is from October to February. The only possible base for a visit is the village of Sawai Madhopur. Its train station is 160 miles (258 km) from Delhi, and it is 7 miles (11 km) from the reserve. There is a rest house in the reserve. The reserve can be visited by car on one-day excursions.

The Bharatpur sanctuary (also known as Keoladeo Ghana) is the most famous protected area for birds in Asia. Many birds nest in the trees of the marsh, including several types of storks, cormorants, spoonbills, ibises, and the sea eagle. Jacana and sultana birds, snakebirds, pelicans, ducks, and other birds are commonly seen at Bharatpur. In the drier areas, there are Antigone cranes. In the winter months, a number of Siberian cranes arrive at the sanctuary (their world population is fewer than four hundred).

Some of the mammal inhabitants are rhesus monkeys, jackals, civets, mongooses, nilgau and reedbuck antelope, and several chital and sambar deer. Pythons are quite common.

Sariska (37)

Sultanpur (38)

NEPAL

Chitwan (39)

BANGLADESH

Chittagong (40)

The nearest airport is at Agra, 30 miles (48 km) away. From there one can reach Bharatpur by bus or car. In addition, there is a convenient train station at Bharatpur 105 miles (169 km) from Delhi. It is only one mile from the lodges that are in the park. Rental boats are available near the lodges.

The Sariska Tiger Reserve is the closest tiger reserve to Delhi. It extends over 300 sq. miles (775 sq. km) of flat land, which is largely covered by deciduous forests. Besides tigers, several leopards, jackals, striped hyenas, rabbits, porcupines, sambar and chital deer, nilgau antelope, Indian gazelles, four-horned antelope, and langur and rhesus monkeys live in this reserve. There are also peacocks, wild cocks, and magpies.

The reserve is located near Alwar on the road that leads to Jaipur, which is about 120 miles (193 km) from Delhi. From the train station at Alwar, one can continue by car to the rest house, which is another 22 miles (35 km).

The Sultanpur reserve is 30 miles (48 km) from Delhi. During the winter, many birds stay in the areas surrounding its lake, including wild geese, ducks, pelicans, flamingos, shorebirds, cormorants, spoonbills, demoiselle cranes, and Antigone cranes. The shores are free of vegetation and offer spectacular views. A comfortable rest house is available on the lakeshore.

The Royal Chitwan National Park is located southwest of Kathmandu, and it includes part of the Churia hills. The park was established in 1973 for the conservation of the one-horned rhinoceros, which is still found in the area.

Other animals include tigers, leopards, lipped bears, gaurs, gavials, and many species of birds. Visitors can find lodgings at Tiger Tops and Jungle Lodge.

The Chittagong Hill Tracts national park includes part of the hills overlooking the mouth of the Ganges River and the Bay of Bengal. This vast territory covers 3,860 sq. miles (10,000 sq. km). It includes several cities, picturesque gorges of the Karnafuli River, teak forests,

and savannas. The animal inhabitants include tigers, elephants, leopards, dhole dogs, and numerous species of birds.

The Sunderbans park is located on the Ganges River delta. Its largest part belongs to Bangladesh. Both India and Bangladesh have set aside this wild marshland as a national park.

Sunderbans (41)

SRI LANKA

Ruhuna (42)

The Ruhuna National Park is situated in the extreme southeast part of the island and is about 190 miles (305 km) from Colombo. It extends over an area of more than 386 sq. miles (1,000 sq. km) and includes jungle, sparse forests, and, toward the sea, large sand dunes. Among the animals of the park are numerous elephants, bears, leopards, chital and sambar deer, wild boars, crocodiles, and more than two hundred species of birds.

Visitors must be accompanied by a professional guide (a free service at the park).

Wilpattu (43)

The Wilpattu National Park is situated 105 miles (170 km) north of Colombo in an area largely covered by dense jungle and small lakes. Bears and leopards are numerous, and several aquatic birds can also be seen. The best period to visit is from May to July.

Gal Oya (44)

The Gal Oya National Park is situated around a vast artificial lake. One-fourth of this area is covered by evergreen forest and the remaining area is primarily a savanna with few trees. Other than the numerous elephants, there are leopards, buffalo, jackals, reptiles, and many aquatic birds.

Kumana, Wirawila, and Bundala (45)

The coastal bird sanctuaries of Kumana, Wirawila, and Bundala are all located on the southeast coast of the island, 135 to 190 miles (217 to 306 km) from Colombo. Its lagoons, marshes, and jungles are inhabited by aquatic and forest birds.

Udawattekele and Peak Wilderness (46)

The mountain sanctuaries of Udawattekele and Peak Wilderness are both about 75 miles (120 km) from Colombo. In addition to interesting forest birds, the area offers some interesting vegetation, such as orchids and rhododendrons.

GLOSSARY

adaptation change or adjustment by which a species or individual improves its condition in relationship to its environment.

agriculture the science and art of farming.

arboreal of or like a tree; living in trees or adapted for living in trees.

biogeography the branch of biology that deals with the geographical distribution of plants and animals.

biology the science that deals with the origin, history, physical characteristics, life processes, etc. of plants and animals.

botanist a plant specialist who studies the science of plants.

canopy anything that covers or seems to cover, like an awning or other rooflike structure. Trees form a canopy in the forest.

carnivore a meat-eating organism such as a predatory mammal, a bird of prey, or an insectivorous plant. The rare Asian lion is a carnivore.

conifers cone-bearing trees and shrubs, most of which are evergreens.

conservation the controlled use and systematic protection of natural resources.

crest a tuft, ridge, or similar growth on the head of a bird or other animal.

cultivate to prepare and use soil or land for growing crops.

deciduous forests forests having trees that shed their leaves at a specific season or stage of growth.

deforestation the clearing of forests or trees.

delta a deposit of sand and soil, usually triangular in shape. Deltas are formed at the mouths of some rivers.

domesticate to tame wild animals and breed them for many purposes. Many European and Asian wild oxen have been domesticated for agricultural purposes.

dominant that species of plant or animal which is most numerous in a community, and which has control over the other organisms in its environment. Dominant species always grow in great numbers.

ecology the relationship between organisms and their environment.

environment the circumstances or conditions of a plant or animal's surroundings.

erosion natural processes such as weathering, abrasion, and corrosion, by which material is removed from the earth's surface.

evolution a gradual process in which something changes into a different and usually more complex or better form.

exotic foreign; not native; strange or different in a way that is striking or fascinating.

extinction the process of destroying or extinguishing.

ganglion a mass of nerve cells serving as a center from which nerve impulses are transmitted.

geology the science dealing with the physical nature and history of the earth.

herbivore an animal that eats plants.

insectivore an animal that eats insects.

latitude the angular distance, measured in degrees, north or south from the equator.

migrate to move from one region to another with the change in seasons.

monsoon a seasonal wind of the Indian Ocean and South Asia, blowing from the southwest from April to October, and from the northeast during the rest of the year.

naturalist a person who studies nature, especially by direct observation of animals and plants.

nocturnal referring to animals that are active at night.

nomads people or animals without a permanent home, who move around constantly in search of food and pasture.

ornithology the branch of zoology dealing with birds.

parasite an organism that grows, feeds, and is sheltered on or in a different organism while contributing nothing to the survival of its host.

peninsula a land area almost entirely surrounded by water and connected to the mainland by a narrow strip of earth called an "isthmus."

physiology the branch of biology dealing with the function and processes of living organisms or their parts and organs.

plateau an elevated and more or less level expanse of land.

plumage the feathers of a bird. A bird's plumage can provide camouflage, aid in identification, and play an important role in mating rituals.

poaching to trespass on private property, especially for hunting or fishing; to hunt or catch game or fish illegally.

pollute to make unclean, impure; contaminate. The delicate balance of nature is often disturbed by pollution.

predator an animal that lives by preying on others.

prey an animal hunted or killed for food by another.

sanctuary a place of refuge or protection; a place where animals or birds are sheltered for breeding purposes and may not be hunted or trapped.

savanna a treeless plain or a grassland characterized by scattered trees, especially in tropical or subtropical regions having seasonal rains.

species a distinct kind, sort, variety, or class. Plant and animal species have a high degree of similarity and can generally interbreed only among themselves.

steppe a large plain having few trees. Many of the steppes in Europe and Asia have been cultivated and planted with grain crops.

subcontinent a large land mass smaller than that usually called a continent; often, a subdivision of a continent, regarded as a geographic or political entity. The Indian subcontinent is one of the most populated zones of the earth.

talon the claw of a bird of prey or other predatory animal. The fish-eating owl has long talons that are well suited for fishing.

terrace a raised, flat mound of earth with sloping sides. The area surrounding India's Deccan plateau forms a series of terraces, hills, and valleys.

terrestrial living on land rather than in water, air, or trees. The Asian elephant is the largest terrestrial animal in Asia.

tributary a small stream which flows into another, larger one.

valley a stretch of low land lying between hills or mountains and usually having a river or stream flowing through it.

vegetarian a person or animal that eats no animal products. Vegetarians have a diet of vegetables, fruit, grains, and nuts.

zoologist a specialist in the study of animals; their life structure, growth, and classification.

INDEX

CREDITS

MAPS AND DRAWINGS. G. Vaccaro, Cologna Veneta (Verona, Italy). **PHOTOGRAPHS. A. Borroni,** Milan: M. Mairani 8. **L. Boitani,** Rome 75. **A. Casdia,** Brugherio (Milan): 16, 20-21, 30, 34, 44-45, 93. **Marka Graphic,** Milan: Atoz Images Inc./Rupinder 80-81; M. Bertinetti 15; Cavalleri 6-7; Globe Photos, Inc./Will 83; T. Zimmermann 76. **G. Mazza,** Montecarlo 26, 42, 53, 56-57, 90. **Panda Photo,** Rome: M. Mariani 94, 96; Archivio Panda 65; F. Pratesi 108-109; WWF International/E.P. Gee 68; WWF International/Y.J. Rey-Millet 40, 48-49; WWF International/Ranjitsinh 84-85. **L. Ricciarini,** Milan: G. Cappelli 25, 70-71; N. Cirani 62; Archivio 2P, Cover photo. **M.P. Stradella,** Milan: Studio Pizzi 66-67, 99. **F. Veronesi,** Segrate (Milan): 11, 14, 18-19, 22-23, 32-33, 35, 36, 38, 50, 54, 60, 86, 92, 102, 114-115, 120-121.